The Complete Guide to Associate and Affiliate Programs on the Net

Turning Clicks into Cash

DANIEL GRAY

McGraw-Hill

New York   San Francisco   Washington, D.C.   Auckland   Bogotá
Caracas   Lisbon   London   Madrid   Mexico City   Milan
Montreal   New Delhi   San Juan   Singapore
Sydney   Tokyo   Toronto

McGraw-Hill

*A Division of The **McGraw·Hill** Companies*

1 2 3 4 5 6 7 8 9 0   AGM / AGM   9 0 9 8 7 6 5 4 3 2 1 0 9

ISBN 0-07-135310-0

This book was set in Palatino by Inkwell Publishing Services.

Printed and bound by Quebecor Martinsburg.

 This book is printed on recycled, acid-free paper containing a minimum of 50% recycled de-inked fiber.

To my friends,
family,
and all the folks who have helped along the way.

This one's for you.

Contents

Introduction

Looking for a way to get in on the Internet boom without risking the ranch? Read on and learn how associate and affiliate marketing programs offer a piece of the ecommerce pie to the little guy. You don't have to be funded by venture capitalists to tap into the clickstream. You just need a dream and the tenacity to make it come true.

WHY I CAME TO WRITE THIS BOOK

I was walking the kids to the bus stop one morning in the fall of 1998. As we strolled up the block, I noticed an unfamiliar minivan making its way down the street. I soon realized that it was a newspaper delivery truck. As the minivan drew closer, I could see that it was a top-of-the-line cruiser—a fully loaded thirty-thousand-something testament to Detroit's commitment to family values. And the driver. The driver was a few years older than I, with a great deal less hair. My mind kicked into overdrive, spinning a tale.

I surmised that this poor fellow had fallen on tough times. For all one knows, he may have been buried in credit card debt or laid off from his cushy corporate job. Maybe he just had a kid or two to put through college (or orthodontics). In any case, he surely wasn't making his mama proud (appreciative, perhaps, but not proud). "That will never happen to me," I thought to myself, as I watched the minivan roll to the end of the block. I tugged at my goatee and mused, "This geek daddy knows better." As the school bus whisked away, I came up with the working title to this book: *Working the Web Sure Beats Getting a Paper Route*. I knew there had to be a better way. And there is.

WHAT ARE ASSOCIATE AND AFFILIATE PROGRAMS?

Associate and affiliate marketing programs allow a merchant Web site to compensate an affiliated Web site for sending traffic. While the dynamics of the Web allow any site to link to any other site without compensation, associate and affiliate programs provide a means for the referring site to profit from referrals that result in a product sale or lead generation. These affiliate commissions can be thought of as finder's fees. Merchants typically pay a percentage of the sale—ranging from 5 to 15 percent, sometimes higher. Accumulated fees are paid to the affiliate site on a monthly, quarterly, or semiannual basis, depending on the program.

Amazon.com is widely accepted as a vanguard of associate marketing. It was one of the first sites to launch an associates program in 1996, and today it boasts over hundreds of thousands of associates. The terms—"associate" and "affiliate"—are generally interchangeable. While Amazon.com popularized the associate term, the majority of merchants refer to their affinity marketing efforts as affiliate programs. This book follows suit.

It's important to differentiate true affiliate marketing programs, which pay a bounty per sale or lead, from similar forms of Internet marketing, which pay for the display of banner advertisements or per click-through. Affiliate marketing offers the biggest bang for the merchant's buck. The merchant pays only when an item is sold or when a valid lead is received. This allows the merchant to create brand awareness through banner advertising without spending a fortune on a conventional advertising campaign. To paraphrase the Dire Straits song, merchants only pay "money for something and get their click-throughs for free."

Affiliate Web sites do not have to pay to join these great programs. Generally, there's no fee; all the checks flow from the merchant to the affiliate. If a program *does* have a sign-up fee, be wary.

WHY YOU NEED THIS BOOK

Is it time for your Web site to earn its keep? Are you interested in affiliate marketing as a way to raise money for a nonprofit organization? Do you need to make the most of your present affiliate efforts? This book cuts through the hype to help you understand how affiliate programs work and how they can best work for you. Despite the claims of certain parties, there are precious few who have become filthy rich from their affiliate Web site. On the other hand, certain sites *have* made a tidy sum. A quick scan of the highest monthly program payouts proves to be enlightening.

In some ways, affiliate marketing hearkens back to the carnival barker. *The Complete Guide to Associate and Affiliate Programs on the Net* serves as your filter, to "optimize your signal-to-noise ratio." There are upwards of a thousand associate and affiliate programs these days, many making claims that would be impossible to achieve, if not incredibly difficult. If you were to believe some of these claims, you'd retire to your own island in the South Pacific in a matter of months.

My goal is to help you think about your Web site in a slightly different light. I want you to consider the site content and audience, along with your immediate and long-term goals. You *can* get where you want to go. You just have to chart your course. If you're to succeed as an affiliate, you must set your expectations reasonably and, most importantly, think strategically about which programs are right for your Web site.

HOW THIS BOOK IS ORGANIZED

This book is organized into seven chapters:

- Chapter 1 explains how affiliate programs work, why they make sense, and how you can make them work for you.

- Chapter 2 provides hints and tips on how to build an effective affiliate site. You'll learn how to build community, select merchants, generate traffic, and add productive links.

- Chapter 3 lays out additional traffic generation strategies, explaining how search engines and other links can send your Web site a steady stream of qualified visitors.

- Chapter 4 tells how to keep track of the statistics—both on your Web server and with the affiliate programs themselves.

- Chapter 5 allows you to peek inside some of the Web's best affiliate programs, with profiles of fourteen merchants.

- Chapter 6 tells real life success stories from affiliate sites around the world. You'll learn what works from the folks who have made it work.

■ Chapter 7 contains the "Top 100 Directory." This directory focuses on quality over quantity, delivering key details on one hundred of the best affiliate programs.

As you read through the merchant profiles and the Top 100 Directory, you will see many well-known names. And for good reason: Brand name familiarity is essential for success on the Web. Do you feel more comfortable purchasing online from a familiar company? I do. There's a good chance your visitors will too.

LIVE OFF THE CLICKSTREAM

The field of affiliate marketing is expanding at warp speed. LinkShare Corporation, the largest provider of affiliate marketing services, reports a fourteenfold increase in their network traffic from the third quarter of 1998 to the third quarter of 1999. So how busy is busy? LinkShare logged a whopping 10 million clicks through their affiliate network links in the third quarter of 1999. "The volume and growth in traffic through The LinkShare Network have been staggering by any measure," said Heidi Messer, president and cofounder of LinkShare. "But the best news is that not only are consumers clicking through more, they're buying more. In Q3 `99, one in fifty click-throughs resulted in a sale, compared to one in 180 during the same period last year. Clearly, that kind of growth and improvement in conversion to sales benefits both merchants and their affiliates. There really couldn't be a better time to become involved in affiliate marketing."

Affiliate marketing is a way to be paid for wearing a T-shirt with a logo. It's the ultimate revenue-sharing extension of the sandwich board. If your dream is to live off the clickstream (or just live a little better), this book helps you get started in the right direction. Don't just jump on the highway. Carefully plan out your route and get the feel for the machinery before hitting the road. Once you've mapped out where you want to go, you can drive knowingly and ride the highway to success.

CHAPTER 1

Why Become an Associate or Affiliate?

As the world adopts online purchasing habits, a fundamental change is taking place in how retailers acquire customers. The new customer acquisition model bypasses the printing industry, it outflanks the post office, and it gives a wink and a nod to traditional media. Consider Amazon.com. In just five short years, the company has rocketed from a garage-based start-up operation to yearly net sales of over $600 million dollars in 1998. Amazon.com was able to make these extraordinary gains in a relatively flat bookselling market.

Associate marketing was part of Amazon.com's huge advantage. The company was able to plaster its name (and, more importantly, its links) on more than 260,000 Web sites (as of April 1999) and bring in the customers without spending an exorbitant amount on a branding campaign.

A FIRST-HAND VIEW

My stock-in-trade is computer how-to books. In the fall of 1997, I decided to launch my own Web site, geekbooks.com, in order to support the books that I had written. I knew that I would have fixed expenses of roughly $25 each month, to cover the Internet Service Provider's (ISP) hosting fees. While not a huge chunk of change, I was already thinking about ways to subsidize the expense.

It didn't take me long to decide to become an Amazon.com associate. It was an obvious leap from simply providing support for my books to actually selling those books through my Web site. Over time, geekbooks.com has consistently generated enough sales to cover my ISP hosting fees. Only now, I don't like to think of it that way. Instead, I like to think that Amazon.com buys a nice dinner, once a quarter.

I didn't take a proactive approach to my bookselling efforts at first. I merely posted a table of contents for each book, along with links to Amazon. After seeing how I was able to generate an income stream with very little effort, I became fascinated with the prospects of affiliate marketing. I realized that affiliate programs represented the adult's version of a child's lemonade stand. The barrier to entry is insignificant. The potential rewards are not.

HOW DOES IT WORK?

Affiliate Web sites are independent entities that have entered into agreements to provide links to merchant Web sites. You might think of this configuration as consisting of a mothership and satellite ships. The satellite sites feed a stream of visitors to the mothership. In an optimized situation, the satellite sites do more than provide click-through; they provide qualified leads.

Let's get right down to it. Affiliate agreements are primarily sales-related. The merchants want something and they are willing to pay a handsome sum to achieve their goals. Usually, they're looking for sales. Sometimes, they're trolling for names to build mailing lists (so that they can sell something at a later date).

The affiliate model casts its line straight at the source, instead of throwing a broad, expensive net. Here's a common scenario. One of your friends is researching the purchase of a new car. Looking for information on a certain make and model of automobile, your friend likely would use a search engine, such as Excite or Lycos, to find Web sites that provide information on that vehicle. Once at those Web sites, the researcher might find pertinent links to an affiliate merchant site. In this case, there might be links to a bookstore to purchase books about the car, to an automotive price quoting service, or to an automotive accessory store.

Types of Programs

There are a number of different types of affiliate marketing programs.

- *Sales commission:* The affiliate site is paid a percentage of each sale. The percentage varies, depending on the merchant's program, type of goods, and any special incentives in force at the time of sale.
- *Customer acquisition:* The affiliate site is paid a fee for each new customer referred to the merchant. The customer acquisition fee may be paid in addition to (or in lieu of) a sales commission.
- *Lead generation:* The affiliate site is paid a fee for each valid lead. These fees vary widely. A request to be added to a mailing list might net the affiliate site a dollar, while a successful credit card application can pull in twenty bucks.
- *Click-through:* The affiliate site is paid for each click-through to the merchant's Web site. Because click-through fees often net only pennies a pop, it takes a significant volume of traffic to make these programs worthwhile for the affiliate site.
- *Impression:* The affiliate is paid a flat fee based on every thousand impressions. Due to the numbers involved, low traffic sites are usually cut out of this more conventional form of Web advertising.

This book focuses on affiliate programs based on sales commission, customer acquisition, and lead generation. While click-through- and impression-based programs may be attractive for high-traffic sites, they do not offer serious income potential for sites across the board. There are some exceptions, as you'll see in the Top 100 Directory, but a highly targeted medium-traffic site will probably be most successful with sales and lead generation programs.

Mechanics

When you sign up with an affiliate program, the merchant provides the means for you to create special links, coded with your account number. You place these links—which may be in the form of banner advertisements, buttons, text links, or even turnkey stores— on your Web pages. Once you've uploaded the Web pages to your Web server, your visitors are able to use the affiliate links. When a visitor clicks on a affiliate-linked banner, button, or text link, special software takes note of the coded link as the new page is served. If a visitor makes a purchase or fulfills a lead as a result of the referral, your account is credited with the appropriate amount.

Payment terms vary from program to program. Most merchants pay their affiliates monthly or quarterly, once the affiliate has reached a prespecified balance in their account. If an affiliate fails to reach the payout level, the funds stay in the account until the level is reached.

Merchants provide affiliate account information via email or private Web sites. Amazon.com, for example, provides weekly and quarterly email reporting, while barnesandnoble.com provides daily reporting via their password-protected affiliate Web site (www.affiliate.net).

WHY DOES AFFILIATE MARKETING MAKE SENSE?

While affiliate marketing was once viewed as an oddity, it has quickly grown into the most important and effective form of Web-based marketing. At its best, affiliate marketing has the weight of a personal recommendation. This viral, word-of-mouth-meets-email approach has accelerated the success of an array of Web-based merchants.

For the Affiliate

The affiliate model gives the little guy a piece of the action. You don't need a huge investment of capital—only some knowledge of the Web's HyperText Markup Language (HTML), the love of a subject, and an understanding of the ways of the Internet. If you can turn what you know into an effective Web site, you can turn that Web site into a moneymaker.

Affiliate programs are about more than just *making* money. They're about *saving* money too. Many affiliate programs allow you to purchase goods through your own affiliate links—effectively paying yourself the affiliate commission. This can lead to substantial savings, especially when the merchant offers exceptionally high referral fees (such as in a promotional period, when rates can be 20 percent or more).

Check the individual program rules *before* you go wild purchasing through your own links. Some merchants take a firm stance on the issue. For example, not only does Amazon *not* pay associates for purchasing through their own links, they also reserve the right to kick associates out of their program. Nonetheless, there are plenty of booksellers that *do* allow their affiliates to earn commission fees on their own purchases.

For the Merchant

Associate programs supersede traditional sales, marketing, and advertising programs. To attract customers in the conventional retail world, a traditional brick-and-mortar store incurs considerable expense. This expense is spread over a number of media:

- Print advertising in local newspapers
- Phone book advertising
- Direct mail collateral
- Radio and television commercials

Once the brick-and-mortar store has lured the customer through the doors, additional resources are applied for floor and window displays. Sales staff have to be walking the floor and behind the cash registers. The floor salesperson answers questions and provides recommendations—all to steer the customer to the right selection.

The Web demolishes that model. Doing business in the virtual world lessens the need for traditional printed advertising. A Web catalog house has no need for a printed catalog. A Web grocery doesn't stuff circulars into your local newspaper. A Web travel agent doesn't depend on full-page advertisements in the phone book.

Of course, in this interim time, traditional advertising media are bursting with www.this and dotcom.that. Web merchants are using conventional media to build their brand awareness. Most of the merchants' televisions commercials, for example, stress corporate identity, rather than driving sales of a specific product.

Researching and buying products on the Web is an entirely different process than in the real world. As a whole, buyers find the products that interest them. This lessens the producer's responsibility to find the buyer. Choices are not limited to what the brick-and-mortar store has featured in its advertising campaign that week.

HOW MUCH MONEY CAN I MAKE?

I'll say it straight out: You won't become wealthy as an affiliate site. If you approach this with a level head, however, you can generate a respectable stream of revenues. You need to set realistic goals.

The potential of your revenue stream is directly related to four things:

- *Impressions:* How many visitors saw the offer?
- *Click-throughs:* How many visitors clicked on the offer?
- *Sales/leads:* How many visitors made a purchase or fulfilled the lead requirements?
- *Value of transaction:* How much will you make from each sale or lead?

The amount of traffic your site generates is of utmost importance. The affiliate program signup forms often ask for monthly page impression counts and unique visitor estimates. As you'll learn in Chapter 4, both figures can be ascertained by analyzing your Web server logs. The number of page impressions is the number of HTML pages served (image hits, such as GIF and JPEG graphics, are ignored). The unique visitor count is calculated by counting the number of different clients who access your server. Some affiliate programs may reject your application if your site traffic is under 10,000 page impressions per month.

The click-through ratio relates the number of link impressions to the number of times the link is followed. For example, if a link is shown 100 times and it is followed 5 times, the link is said to have a click-through ratio of 5 percent. Click-through ratios vary widely. The effectiveness of your links cannot be understated. You won't strike it rich when you throw up a page full of banner ads. It just doesn't happen. (Chapter 2 delves into the subject of linking.)

The conversion of click-through to sales or leads is a key point. The relevancy of your site content to the affiliate offers is crucial. Don't attempt to sell cosmetics or panty hose to truck drivers. Send potential customers to your merchants. Don't focus just on traffic; instead, focus on quality.

At this point, you might be asking yourself, "Well, that's all great, but how much money can I really make?" I can't answer that with a generalization. Your site is unique. You're the one who has to decide how much money you expect to make. The approach you take and the tactics you use are infinitely variable.

Let's put the answer in fishing terms. Some fish swim by (impressions), some fish take the bait (click-throughs), and some fish end up as dinner (sales/leads). The fatter the fish (the value of the transaction), the less fish you need to put on the table. Once you've led your fish to the bait, you want them to take it. The value of the transaction and the frequency of transactions are essential to your profitability. Do you want to make 5 percent of a $500 sale a few times a month? Or would you be happier generating dozens of $2 referrals? A couple of big tuna or an ice chest full of trout? It's all up to you.

Here's a relatively discouraging chart. Assume 10,000 impressions per month, a click-through rate of 1 percent (not unreasonable with banner ads), a conversion rate of 1 percent, an average sale of $30, and a 15 percent commission fee. In a month's time, this site would generate a whopping $4.50—not enough to buy a plate of fish and chips.

Impressions	Click-through	Conversion	Average Sale	Commission
	(1%)	(1%)	($30)	(15%)
10,000	100	1	Total sales of $30	Affiliate revenue $4.5

Don't get bummed out yet. Let's take that same 10,000-impression site, but add a targeted stream of traffic. If you hit your audience with the right offer and effective links, you can goose your click-through. Even with the same conversion rate, you begin to yield a respectable sum. You can go out for a nice dinner with the family.

Impressions	Click-through	Conversion	Average Sale	Commission
	(25%)	(1%)	($30)	(15%)
10,000	2,500	25	Total sales of $750	Affiliate revenue $112.50

Let's take one more spin through the numbers. This time, the site is serving 40,000 impressions per month, with a click-through rate of 12 percent, a conversion rate of 1 percent, an average sale of $500, and a 5 percent commission fee. Still wondering how you're going to put little Jimmy through college?

Impressions	Click-through	Conversion	Average Sale	Commission
	(12%)	(1%)	($500)	(5%)
40,000	2,500	48	Total sales of $24,000	Affiliate revenue $1,200

This should give you an idea of what's possible. While we could go on with hypothetical charts, plugging in your own numbers is actually more fun. If you're halfway handy with a spreadsheet program, you can construct a little calculator to play with the figures. Or you can download a sample spreadsheet from my Website (www.geekbooks.com).

Now let's take a look at the real world. I polled over 100 companies in the process of writing this book. A little more than a quarter of them were willing to release figures for their highest monthly affiliate commissions. Table 1-1 shows the highest payouts to single affiliates.

Some program managers couldn't reveal the exact amount, but were willing to share rough figures or friendly generalizations. QSPACE said "a few thousand dollars," while FreeShop said "several thousand dollars." Fogdog Sports said, "Can't say, but it's high," while Reel.com happily chimed that their highest monthly payout was "enough to keep them swimming in new videos."

WHAT'S THE BEST PROGRAM FOR MY SITE?

Of the hundreds of affiliate and associate programs, perhaps a handful are suitable for your Web site. Your site content and audience dictate the most appropriate programs. I'm not going to pick out a top ten list or insist that you have to join a particular program. But most affiliates have found certain guidelines helpful.

Books Sell!

The simple fact is that people buy books online. Consequently, the bookstore programs have been the first step into the world of affiliate marketing for many a Web site. If you're ready to make your initial foray, sign up with one of the name brand merchants. Look at the programs carefully before you decide between barnesandnoble.com, 1BookStreet, Fatbrain, Borders, Amazon, and the others. Where would *you* want to shop? Pick the store and program that best fits your site. When you execute your site bookstore correctly, you can make money with *any* of the big booksellers. But you can make *more* from some than others.

The booksellers differ in a number of ways, other than in commission terms. Fatbrain has an exclusively technical focus, while 1BookStreet specializes in out-of-print and bargain titles. Also, barnesandnoble.com sells software and pays commission on gift certificates (while other programs may not).

Table 1-1—Highest Monthly Commission Paid to Date

LendingTree	$97,000
TransAct! Offer Network	$20,000
One & Only Network	$19,000
NextCard Internet Visa	$17,760
Autoweb.com	$10,000+
ArtToday	$5,000
Astrology.net's ChartShop	$5,000+
Liquor By Wire	$3,000
FirstPlace Software, Inc.	$2,500
CarPrices.com	$2,200
Enews (formerly Electronic Newsstand)	$2,000
Fatbrain.com	$2,000
The LobsterNet	$1,800
Web Cards	$1,500
Verio Affiliates Program	$1,025
BabyCenter.com	$1,000
Proflowers.com	$1,000+
HotHotHot.com	$1,000
Seattle's Finest Gourmet Coffee	$950
Network Solutions	$2,234/quarter
Underneath.com	$600
1BookStreet.com	$600
Chipshot.com	$370
Shades.com	$350
Swiss Army Depot	$325
Epage	$314.43
SmarterKids.com	$252.44
Internet News Bureau	$200
Genius Babies!	$200
i/us: all things graphic	$455/quarter
Barewalls.com	$150
Simon's Stamps	$107
CBS SportsLine	Approximately $150
XOOM.com	$75
OutdoorDecor.com	$63.51

Give Something Away

Lead generation campaigns can be extremely effective revenue generators for the affiliate site. Unlike sales offers, the visitor is asked to give little more than their name, address, and perhaps some demographic information. There's no pressure for the visitor to whip out a credit card, and there's no denying the allure of the freebie. As you flip through the pages of the Top 100 Directory, you'll find excellent per-lead affiliate programs from AutoWeb.com, CarPrices.com, FreeShop, and TransAct. Take a look at the payouts in Table 1-1; these affiliate programs are among the most potent on the Web today.

Select Carefully

While upward of a thousand affiliate programs are out there, for you the vast majority of them do not matter! When I set out to create *The Complete Guide to Associate and Affiliate Programs on the Net* Top 100 Directory, I made the decision to emphasize the best affiliate programs on the Web: programs with recognizable, responsible merchants—companies with name recognition, good management, and stable footing. I wasn't looking to compete with the burgeoning Web-based affiliate program directories (see Chapter 4). My goal was to cut through the clutter by providing *more* information about *fewer* companies.

At its best, affiliate marketing can be thought of as a partnership between the affiliate and the merchant. This agreement should be much more than just an advertising relationship. When you choose your merchants, you're choosing the partners you'll take on your ride down the river. If the river gets slow, you want to know that they can paddle. And if the boat tips over, you want to know that they can swim.

Most of all, you want to know that the merchants will deliver on their promises. Don't be wooed by fast talk. Look at the facts. What's the potential for affiliate revenue? Take your site history into account and run the numbers through this simple equation:

$$\text{Impressions} \times \text{Click-through} \times \text{Conversion} \times \text{Average sale} \times \text{Commission} = \text{Potential revenue}$$

Relevancy

Choosing only the most relevant programs can take discipline. A merchant with higher relevancy and a lower commission schedule is a better bet than a merchant with low relevancy and higher commissions.

Relevancy drives both click-through and conversion. Always keep in mind that:

- Your site must have something interesting to say.
- Information must be well presented.
- Links must be in context.
- A conversion rate of 1 percent is nothing to sneeze at.

To maximize your revenue potential, select the merchant(s) carrying the products that are most appropriate for your site.

WHO ARE THE PLAYERS?

Affiliate programs are administered in two ways. They're either run inhouse by the merchant, or the program is outsourced to a third-party affiliate program service bureau. Amazon, Beyond.com, and CDNOW are among the largest programs administered inhouse. Of the handful of players in the service bureau business, the biggest are Be Free, Linkshare, Commission Junction, and Microsoft's ClickTrade. The bulk of top-tier third-party merchant programs are administered by Be Free and Linkshare. Recent entries into the affiliate service bureau market include PlugInGo (http://www.plugingo.com) and Nexchange (http://www.nexchange.com).

Be Free—www.befree.com

Be Free, Inc. was founded in January 1996 by Tom and Sam Gerace. The Gerace brothers built a model that uses a merchant-branded network, where the merchant owns the network. The tone was set for the Massachusetts-based company when they launched the barnesandnoble.com affiliate network in the summer of 1997. Be Free soon added enews.com and Travelocity to their stable of merchants. While Be Free began by building exclusive merchant-branded programs, they're moving toward a more open model. Be Free's FastApp allows affiliates to apply for more than one program at a time. Their affiliates select an average of 1.6 programs when they apply. As of September 1999, the company provided services for more than 160 merchants with over 1.6 million affiliates.

Be Free merchants include American Greetings, Baby Center, barnesandnoble.com, Carclub.com, CarPrices.com, Chip Shot Golf, Consumers Car Club, eBags.com, enews.com, Fogdog Sports, Getsmart, Giftpoint.com, GoTo, i/us, LendingTree, MotherNature, Network Solutions, PlanetRx, Priceline.com, Proflowers, Qspace, Reel, Send Wine, Staples, Travelocity.com, Value America, and Xoom.

LinkShare—www.linkshare.com

LinkShare was founded in 1996 by the brother and sister team of Stephen and Heidi Messer. Together with chief technical officer Horace Mang, the Messers launched an open affiliate network with consolidated reporting. Omaha Steaks, Avon, Shades.com, LandscapeUSA, and the Smoke Shop were among LinkShare's first clients. As of September 1999, the New York City–based company provides services to more than 350 merchants and tens of thousands of individual affiliate sites. Unlike the Be Free model, LinkShare owns the network. LinkShare's affiliates are partnering with an average of four programs.

LinkShare merchants include 1-800-Flowers, 1BookStreet.com, Audio Book Club, Avon, Borders.com, CBS SportsLine, Cyberian Outpost, dELiA*s, Dell, Electronics.net, Fashionmall.com, Fragrance Counter, FragranceNet, FreeShop, Green Marketplace, HostAmerica, International Golf Outlet, JCPenney, K-Tel, L'eggs Products, Liquor By Wire, More.com, NextCard Visa, OfficeMax.com, Omaha Steaks, Publishers Clearing House, Shades.com, Sharper Image, SmarterKids.com, Sparks.com, Swiss Army Depot, The Golf Warehouse, Verio/TABNet, and Wine.com.

Commission Junction—www.cj.com

Lex Sisney launched Commission Junction in 1998, as an affordable alternative to Be Free and LinkShare, after running an affiliate merchant program. While Commission Junction primarily services a bevy of small to medium-sized merchants, they're moving upward, having recently added Tower Records and Fingerhut to their roster. As of September 1999, the Santa Barbara, California–based company serviced over 125 merchants, with approximately 150,000 affiliate-to-merchant relationships. Commission Junction is similar to LinkShare in that it operates an open network of merchants, but it goes one better by maintaining combined affiliate accounts. Affiliates are paid by Commission Junction with one check each month, assuming that the affiliate has earned over $25.

Commission Junction merchants include 2 Grrrls, Adguide's College Recruiter Employment Site, Andy's Garage, Animation Factory, Astrology.Net, Books-For-Cooks.com, ClassMates Online, Fingerhut.com, GiftTree, golfstore.com, MountainZone.com, and PC Flowers & Gifts.com.

ClickTrade—www.clicktrade.com

ClickTrade is part of the Microsoft behemoth, although, like many other Microsoft entities, it didn't start out that way. The firm was first acquired by LinkExchange, just prior to LinkExchange's being acquired by Microsoft. The bulk of ClickTrade merchants offer per-click programs, although there are a good number of sales and lead commission programs. Some merchants use both ClickTrade and other affiliate channels. Like Commission Junction, ClickTrade offers consolidated affiliate accounts, with monthly payouts once the account balance reaches $25. ClickTrade merchants include Bottom Dollar Shopping Agent, CarPrices.com, FreeShop, Lobster Net, MySimon, and Simon's Stamps.

It's Alive!

At their best, affiliate programs help to create an evangelistic swell, building on themselves. "Affiliates are like individual organisms, with unique characteristics and traits," said Tom Gerace of Be Free. "With the proper food and water from their merchants—feedback, techniques, information—they become a colony of thriving organisms. Individual affiliates learn in their own lifetime, through their online reporting and commissions. New generations of affiliates and techniques refine the species." Rest assured, as you continue through this book, you'll evolve as an affiliate.

CHAPTER TWO

Building Your Affiliate Site

The key components of a successful affiliate site are clear. You must provide great content that is properly showcased in a clean design. The site must generate sufficient traffic to drive a steady flow of qualified consumers to a targeted set of merchants, through carefully placed links. In short, you want the right people, at the right place, at the right time.

The carnival midway look doesn't cut it. A page that consists merely of flashy banners and animated buttons is an invitation to failure. Your site needs to have purpose. Many affiliate program managers turn down applications from sites that consist solely of ad banners and buttons. These sites rarely perform well as affiliates and in many cases do more harm than good to the brand.

PROVIDING GREAT CONTENT

An affiliate Web site has to have a reason for being—not just for you, but for your visitors. If there's no reason for your visitors to come to your site, there's no reason for your site to exist. Always remember that your visitors are coming to your site for its content, not for the site's affiliate links.

Great original content fills a need for something that is not commonplace on the Web. If your site has been up and running for a while, you should have a handle on audience expectations. If your site is new, you may do well to search out uncharted territory and topics. If you can, do something that hasn't been done (or done *well*) before, you have a chance to get out in front of the pack, while gaining some form of notoriety.

Do It from the Heart

If you're passionate about the subject matter of your Web site, your devotion will show in the content. Money, in the form of affiliate program revenue, should not be your primary motivating factor when setting up the Web site. If you love what you do, you'll be successful no matter how much you earn. The Webmasters of successful affiliate sites are like attentive gardeners: For a site to flourish, it must be planted, watered, pruned, fertilized, and weeded. The more time you spend tending your Web garden, the larger and more productive it becomes.

Encourage Community

Healthy Web sites encourage a sense of community. Think of the people who come to your site as members of that community, not as faceless nodes on the network. Community features such as newsletters, mail lists, and bulletin boards increase site *stickiness*. You can use these features to establish your community and provide an environment that fosters increased page views. Give folks a warm, friendly, and informative place on the Web and they'll keep coming back for more. Each time your community members return, they'll become more familiar with your affiliate offers, and the more likely that they will eventually click-through and make a purchase.

How many times have you walked right into a brand new shop and made a purchase on the spot? I'm more likely to take a look around on that first visit to a new store. If a product catches my eye, I'll stop back in and buy that product on a return visit.

Newsletters

Email newsletters (sometimes referred to as *announcement lists*) provide an ideal vehicle to get the word out to community members. With an email newsletter, you can regularly let people know what's happening on your site. While newsletters are primarily a one-way form of communication, with all of the information flowing from the sponsor, they provide the most direct means to drive traffic back to your site. Even better, you can drive traffic directly to your affiliate merchants via links in your email newsletter.

You must be responsible in your email newsletter efforts. Newsletters should always be opt-in, never unsolicited. Unsolicited commercial email (UCE), more commonly referred to as *spam*, is annoying to most recipients and for that reason is highly discouraged. Opt-in newsletters must be requested by the recipient. This subscription model helps to ensure that the newsletter is sent only to those who truly wish to receive it. (Merchants can drop you from their affiliate programs if you send out UCE that contains links to their Web site.) Common "netiquette" dictates that you provide a link to a page explaining how to unsubscribe from the newsletter. This link should be carried at either the top or bottom of the email.

While email affiliate links can be highly effective, unwary list operators run the risk of the appearance of spamming. Don't let this happen to you! Keep your newsletter on target:

- *Control your circulation*. Make sure you're sending the newsletter only to those who have requested it.
- *Keep the content in the forefront*. Remember that your affiliate links are secondary in importance to your readers.
- *Don't load up on affiliate links*. Choose your offers carefully and use them sparingly.
- *Post a privacy policy*. Place a page on your Web site that states exactly what you will and will not do with the names you collect.

You don't have to be a UNIX geek to set up an opt-in email newsletter. A number of companies provide turnkey email newsletter subscription and delivery services. Be sure to look for a program where *you* control any advertising. You may have to fork over some cash to avoid the third-party advertising, but it's well worth it. (The free mailing services make their money from those advertising links.) Here are some likely candidates:

- WebPromote Engage—http://engage.webpromote.com

- LinkExchange ListBot—http://www.listbot.com
- Lyris—http://www.lyris.net

Mail Lists

Mail lists (sometimes referred to as *discussion groups* or *discussion lists*) provide an immediate means of two-way communication among members of the community. When a member of the mail list sends a post to the list, the server distributes the post to every list subscriber. List subscribers can receive posts in as many as four ways (depending on the server):

- *Individual posts*. The posts are received one-by-one, as they are sent.
- *Digest*. The posts are received in bulk, either once a day or more frequently, depending on the volume of list traffic. The individual posts are compiled into one email, in chronological order.
- *Summary*. A summary email, containing email topics and senders, is sent out once a day (or more frequently, depending on traffic). Subscribers can then view only the posts that interest them via a Web interface.
- *Web interface*. The posts are viewed via a convenient Web site. This allows for easy browsing and reference. Subscribers can search list archives online, rather than digging through their own email archives.

The digest, summary, and Web interface methods may offer opportunities for the inclusion of affiliate links as long as your mailing list software allows for this. Digest and summary emails can include unobtrusive links at the bottom of the email. While it would be obnoxious to attach affiliate links to the footer of individual emails, they shouldn't be considered rude when appended to the bottom of either a digest or summary.

Here are some popular mailing list services:

- ONElist—http://www.onelist.com
- Lyris—http://www.lyris.net
- eGroups—http://www.egroups.com

Bulletin Boards

Bulletin boards (often called *discussion forums*) are beautiful. They enable self-generating content that allows a Web site to grow, without the site owner investing a gargantuan effort. As your site grows, so too will the number of affiliate linking opportunities. A well-run bulletin board has a snowball effect. The more posts, the more pages, the more bait for the search engine spiders. This results in more search engine listings, more traffic, and more posts—all boosting the number of impressions while nurturing your community-building efforts.

The bulletin board pages should feature some banner or button affiliate advertising, in addition to affiliate text links. Banner advertisements should not be static; they should rotate throughout the bulletin board pages. You don't want your community members to see the same banner ad on page after page as they navigate through your bulletin board. Banners, like site content, need to be kept fresh.

There are a number of shareware (and freeware) bulletin board CGI (Common Gateway Interface) scripts floating around the Web. If you're looking for a more robust discussion forum (and have a more robust budget), Ultimate Bulletin Board (http://www.ultimatebb.com), Web Crossing (http://www.webcrossing.com), and O'Reilly Software's WebBoard (http://webboard.ora.com) are among the most popular commercial offerings.

Classified Ads and Auctions

Web classified ads and auctions are two great forms of self-generating content. They can also be a nice source of affiliate revenue. EPage (http://ep.com) allows you to put a turnkey classified or auction section onto your Web site for free. The EPage Classified Service Provider program pays affiliate commission fees of up to 30 percent. The One & Only Network (http://www.oneandonlynetwork.com), which specializes in personal classifieds as well as auction classifieds, boasts some of the highest performing affiliate sites on the Web. One & Only pays a 15 percent commission fee, as well as commissions on Webmaster referrals. Both EPage and One & Only were among the earliest affiliate marketing programs on the Web.

While these companies control the advertising space within the pages they serve for your site, you may be able to carry their pages within a framed layout. (It's best to check the individual operating agreement for any restrictions.) Nonetheless, you'll probably want to include affiliate links on any doorway pages that lie in front of the classified pages.

MERCHANT SELECTION

The proper selection of affiliate merchants is a crucial step. You should always strive to select merchants and products that complement the content of your Web site. Affiliate links work best when they come as word of mouth, rather than advertising. To be genuine (and effective), you need to spend time getting to know your product line. There are no shortcuts. You need to research your subject. Once you know what you are selling, you'll become more successful when you evangelize, rather than hawk.

It's a Personal Recommendation

Know your merchants. Don't recommend a product or company you wouldn't recommend to a friend. Test your programs out by buying a little something through your merchant links—make sure that it's *easy* to buy. What was the experience like? If the merchant provides a painless purchase process, excellent service, and customer support (in the form of purchase and shipping confirmation email messages), they've passed the first test.

Did the goods arrive on time? Were they as promised? If so, you can give the merchant a green light. If not, you should proceed with caution or move onto the next merchant. If the goods did not arrive on time or did not meet your expectations, you should follow up with the merchants immediately. The customer service the merchants provide in response to your inquiry helps you to assess whether you want to keep them or drop them. The best merchants come shining through in these situations.

Program Details

Pay close attention to how the merchant's affiliate program is structured. The tools and policies they offer are a factor when weighing a merchant against its competitors. The reporting procedures, payment schedules, revenue potential, and linking process are of primary concern.

- *What's their reporting like?* If you're into statistics, quick feedback, and analytical tools, you'll want an online report like those offered through Be Free, Linkshare, and others. Online reporting lets you see what's happening on a daily basis. This allows you to continually fine-tune your efforts. Weekly email reporting works just fine for those situations where you don't feel the need to keep your hand on the throttle.

- *How do they pay?* Nothing beats getting a check every month. Check to see whether the merchant pays on a monthly or quarterly basis. The minimum payout amount should be reasonable, given the traffic you generate. Commission Junction and ClickTrade are attractive in this regard, as they offer consolidated payments for their merchant customers. Watch out for programs that set an unreasonably high payout level; unless you generate a high level of sales, the merchant's checks will be few and far between.

- *Is the offer worthwhile?* You may love a merchant and you may love the products, but if the commission schedule stinks, you'll do well to pass. Run the numbers through the revenue potential equation outlined back in Chapter 1.

- *What kinds of links do they offer?* Avoid programs that offer only banner advertisements with links to the merchant's front door. You want to drive potential customers right to the products you recommend.

- *How are links generated?* Look for a clean, simple linking procedure. It can be a hassle to cobble your own links together. Short URLs are also important. Long URLs often break in email messages, causing headaches for the potential customer, the merchant, and the affiliate alike.

There are huge differences between the philosophies and resources offered by each merchant. The best run programs foster the relationship between the merchant and the affiliate. "Pay your affiliates and pay them well, but don't just pay them in revenue," said David Pollet Director, Internet Marketing for LendingTree. "Share your content, your tools, your functionality. Invite your affiliate in as a partner and play a critical role in their success." When the merchant treats the affiliate as a colleague, rather than as a subordinate, wonderful things can happen.

Use the Boot

Once you've added a merchant program to your site and given their program a fair shake, you needn't be afraid to boot the merchant if things fail to work out. Give the program plenty of time and impressions to prove itself. Experiment with different types of banners and text links. You'll give away thousands (or tens of thousands) of impressions before being able to make an honest assessment. If a program does not make the grade, remove it and replace it with a new program. Don't waste your space with programs that do not perform.

EFFECTIVE DESIGN

An effectively designed affiliate Web site makes it as easy as possible for visitors to click through to the merchant. Design your site around the content, building the affiliate links into the structure of the page. Don't rely on banner advertisements alone. Instead, use them in concert with consistent text links. While text links score higher click-through ratios, banner advertisements help to achieve merchant branding and name recognition. Your site should be easy to find. Design your pages so that they are search engine–friendly. (See Chapter 3 for more information on search engines.)

Productive Linking Methods

It's essential to experiment with link placement and different linking methods. The difference between click-through and conversion rates can be astounding.

- *Banner links.* The ubiquitous ad banner produces the lowest click-through rates, yet is essential to establish branding. Good programs offer attractive banner ads and buttons in a number of IAB/CASIE standard banner sizes, such as 468×60, 234×60, 120×240, 120×90, 120×60, 125×125, and 88×31. The best programs offer automatic banner rotation.

- *Search box links.* These offer a convenient way for your visitors to find *exactly* what they are looking for on your affiliate merchant's Web site. Search box links pay a lower commission fee with some programs (such as Amazon's 5 percent indirect hit fee). The ingenious folks at Anaconda.net have come up with a method to turn your Web site's Amazon search results into full commission links (15 percent). Their Anaconda CGI script promises to triple the potential earnings from search box hits.

- *Text links*. Simple text links are one of the most effective methods of linking. It's best to keep things on the up and up, however. If you let folks know that you are sending them to an affiliated merchant, it may be possible to achieve a higher sales conversion ratio than if you send them there blindly.

- *Product links*. These links are golden. The combination of a product image and explanatory text can be highly compelling. When visitors click through directly to the product page on the merchant's site, they're primed with information.

- *Turnkey store and merchandizer links*. Found in selected high-end programs offered through Linkshare and Be Free, these instant stores (and banners) can deliver a nice selection of products in a timely manner, while minimizing the effort it takes for you to build your Web store.

- *Email links*. When used in the proper manner, email links are very productive. Once again (and this is worth repeating over and over), you should never send out spam. You might email your friends and family with a cool offer, but you should think twice before posting to a mail list, lest you end up being charbroiled in flames or kicked off the list.

Make sure that your visitors will see your links immediately when they land on a page. Avoid creating layouts that use fixed widths wider than 600 pixels. If you place a link outside that area, folks browsing with low-resolution (640 × 480) displays will not see your links without scrolling horizontally. Keep the vertical dimensions in mind too. Place your most important links toward the top of each Web page, as shown by Figure 2-1. Don't expect that folks will scroll down to find the links.

Sticky Shopping

Don't let your visitors get away too easily. Your site should be as sticky as possible (without being irritating). Two design tricks keep visitors on your site when they follow one of your links: frames and new windows. A framed layout displays the merchant's site within your site's frameset. Frames should be used only if your affiliate merchant agreement allows their use. Framed layouts are not attractive bait for the search engines, however; so you should keep their use to a minimum. Figure 2-2 demonstrates one example of a framed store layout.

Figure 1-1 Think about that daily newspaper. Place your key links above the fold.

24

Figure 2-2 In this example, the merchant site loads in the large bottom frame, while your site maintains navigation via the skinny upper frame.

The best method is to open a new browser window when your visitor clicks on an affiliate link. The linked page opens in the new window, while the original page remains open in the first window. This is the most common way to stay on your visitor's desktop; it's a widespread practice and relatively unobtrusive solution to the issue. Figure 2-3 provides an example of a new merchant window opening via an affiliate link.

Ease of Maintenance

You don't want your affiliate links to become a nightmare to maintain. Design your pages so that the links can be easily updated. Make things as modular as possible and add comments to your HTML code as necessary. While you can use a WYSIWYG Web page editor—such as Microsoft FrontPage, Macromedia Dreamweaver, Adobe PageMill, or GoLive—to create and maintain your Web site, you'll probably paste in your links in HTML source mode. Of course, you don't need expensive Web page editing software to create an effective affiliate site. A good text editor and some knowledge of HTML will see you through.

TRAFFIC GENERATION

Some affiliate programs reject low-traffic Web sites. Others blindly approve an application without regard for traffic volume. In setting a traffic requirement, a merchant is merely playing the numbers: Slow sites have a far lower chance of being productive affiliates, often requiring more attention than their revenue potential may warrant.

It's your responsibility to generate that traffic. Once you've established your Web site with solid content, you need to turn your attention to the gates and let the world know that the site exists. Without a sufficient number of visitors traveling through your gates, the site will never produce a reliable stream of revenue. If you attract the right crowd, you will ensure a steady flow of qualified visitors. What if Walt Disney had kept Disneyland a secret?

The three primary means of external traffic generation are advertising, publicity, and search engine listings.

Advertising

What does your budget look like? While there are many forms of advertising, a great deal are out of reach for the common affiliate Web site.

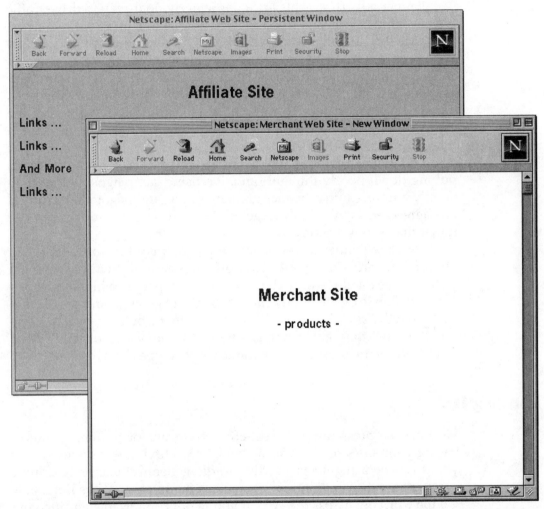

Figure 2-3 Popping up a new window is simple. Just add a TARGET="new" within the link's tag.

The chance that you'll be able to recoup the additional costs of conventional advertising is slim. In most cases, increased affiliate commission fees do not justify the expense.

Banner advertisements are a particularly poor way to drive traffic to your affiliate Web site—poor in two ways. First, they offer poor performance for the dollar, and, second, you'll spend yourself poor before you see any result. Banner exchange schemes, such as LinkExchange, can put your banners on lots of other sites, but you'll have to run their banners in kind. Do you really want to run those banners on your pages? Does the increased traffic (if any) justify the disruption of the purity of your site? Is there a reason to give up control over the presentation of your design?

I don't mean to put down banner advertising as a whole. But I am putting down poorly thought-out advertising campaigns. Rather than blindly entering into a banner exchange program, negotiate reciprocal link agreements with highly targeted sites that can send you prime beef, rather than ground chuck.

Per-click banner advertising campaigns may be worthwhile, but only if you can administrate your affiliates carefully while keeping a watchful eye for click-through fraud. There *are* people with nothing better to do than to create phony click-throughs to generate income. Go figure! Nonetheless, you should make sure that you're paying a click-through rate that is commensurate with the value of the visitor. ClickTrade is the most popular venue for this type of advertising.

Publicity

Working the press can be a cost-effective means of traffic generation. Seeing your site's name in print can be a gratifying experience; better yet, it can be a highly productive traffic generator. Consider using a press release distribution service, such as the Internet News Bureau, to get the word out across the Web. If you're not comfortable writing your own press release, find someone to help. A poorly written press release ends up in the editor's trash bin. A well-written and intriguing release may land significant press coverage.

I spent a whopping year and a half as a marketing communications manager (okay, I was really a PR flak). It was a valuable experience for me, and far less painful than I imagined. Here are some rules of thumb I learned over time:

- *Make it newsworthy*. Don't send out a press release that merely announces your new Web site. No one cares about that! Instead, explain your site's value by telling the editors what your Web site does for its visitors.

- *Tone down the hype*. While a press release isn't a news story, it shouldn't be advertising copy either.

- *Include a quote or two*. Once again, the quotes should not consist of overblown hype. Give the press something that they might actually be able to use.

- *Timing is everything*. Don't send your press releases out too early. They should never go out until the paint is dry and all the "Under Construction" signs have been stowed away.

- *Check it twice*. Double-check that all of the URLs mentioned in the press release are functioning.

- *It's not perfect (yet)*. Don't rely on your spell checker. Have at least two people proofread the press release (other than the person who wrote it).

- *Be thorough*. Contact information should include both a telephone number and an email address. Make sure that the contact person has voice mail. You don't want to miss a call.

- *Call back*. Respond to press inquiries as soon as possible. It's best if someone is standing by the ready when the release is distributed (even though it may take some time for the inquiries to commence). Don't let messages go unreturned.

- *Be easy to deal with*. It's good to be kind and genuine with the press. These folks are often under enormous deadline pressure.

- *Don't be a pest*. Give the press what they need and go away (but follow up as necessary).

- *Be patient*. It can take time for the press release to get the right people. Some editors will run your URL without ever bothering to contact you.

- *Think ahead*. Get that haircut *before* you send out the press release. Hey, you never know!

Michael Smith can attest to the power of Internet press releases. His Great Britain–based company, HotBox (http://www.hotbox.co.uk), is a new Web and mail order retailer of cutting-edge toys and gadgets.

They've positioned themselves as the source for the hottest trends—not just as a retailer, but also as a media resource. "Of all the promotions and marketing we've done for the Web site, the press release sent through the Internet News Bureau brought HotBox the biggest increase in traffic," said Michael. The company saw their unique visitor count explode from an average between 100 and 200 a day all the way up to between 1,000 and 2,000.

How did one press release lead to a ten-fold increase in Web site traffic? "As a result of the press release, HotBox was covered in publications from Argentina, Australia, and across Europe," explained Michael. "Then ABC News called to cover the launch party of our latest product, the Eternity Puzzle." The ABC News coverage was featured on many local ABC News television broadcasts. Publicity snowballed with radio and increased media coverage in print and on the Web. Page views and product sales peaked the day the ABC News coverage hit, with 3,500 visitors and 180 sales. While the numbers leveled off in the following days, traffic and sales have remained strong. "The amount we spent was small change compared to the advantage we got out of it," said Michael.

The event helped to solidify HotBox's stature as an identifier of new trends. Through the publicity, the company was able to increase the circulation of its opt-in newsletter and establish relationships with members of the press relevant to their product offerings. The increased awareness created by the newsletter will enable HotBox to retain customers and media attention as it builds on its success.

Search Engine and Directory Listings

Until your site is well-established, the search engines (such as Infoseek, AltaVista, and HotBot) and directory listings (like Yahoo!) will likely be your primary source of traffic. It is absolutely essential that your site be designed and executed so that it can be fully indexed. The next chapter is devoted entirely to the subject of search engines.

CHARITY FUNDRAISING

Charity fundraising sites are perfect for affiliate marketing. A percentage of each sale goes straight to the nonprofit organization. Imagine if you could shop that way in the real world! The widespread adoption of affiliate marketing will change how nonprofit organizations raise money. It will become common practice to shop through these links. Donations will become part of the daily shopping routine. There will be no need to write a separate check. No reason for those pesky phone calls (that always seem to come during dinner).

Organizations can tailor their selection of merchants to meet specific goals. Fundraising efforts can be tuned to a campaign or issue. Let's look at some scenarios:

- *It's the holiday season.* How about avoiding that annual rush to purchase gifts for friends, family, and loved ones? Instead of pushing your way through the hordes of shoppers in the mall, log onto the Web site of your house of worship or favorite charity to do your shopping? Knowing that a percentage of each sale is sent directly to the charity makes gift giving much more heartwarming.

- *Play ball!* The kids have just signed up for soccer or baseball. Wouldn't it be cool to purchase their sports equipment over the Internet? You might shop from a preapproved list of mitts, bats, cleats, and protective gear—knowing that other parents have checked out the goods in advance. This eliminates the hassle of driving from store to store to find *exactly* the right product. And it can send a new source of funds right to your soccer club or baseball league.

- *The school book fair without walls (or hours).* With a virtual book fair, there's no waiting for the trailer to arrive at your grammar school. Your teachers can pick their favorite books each month. You don't have to rush around to make it to the book fair before dinner. The PTA can schedule one less bake sale.

If you're thinking about creating a charity fundraising affiliate site, the more power to you! I believe that this is one of the most beautiful aspects of the affiliate marketing revolution. To be effective, you have to plan and promote carefully, although the Web site does not have to be extravagant or large. This is one place where the simple shopping mall of affiliate text links can make good sense.

So how do you get the word out to the membership?

- Include information about the online fundraising effort in your printed newsletters. Always remember to include the URL with each article.

- Postcards can be a highly cost-effective form of promotion. They're inexpensive to print and mail. Have someone design a really attractive postcard, and it stays on the refrigerator for months (held up there with a refrigerator magnet from www.fridgedoor.com, of course). Think about having a color postcard made from your beautiful Web site (www.printing.com).

- Send out informative email (not spam!) to your members. Include links to your storefront. You might also include affiliate links directly to the merchants.

- Write up a press release to send to the media. Your local newspaper and radio station are ideal candidates. (With a local campaign, you needn't invest in a press release broadcast.)

Who Builds the Site?

If you have Web-savvy folks in your organization, you'll have a ready source of volunteers. Don't let enthusiasm be a substitute for good design skills, however. While the pages don't need to look like they came from a cutting edge Web design firm, they do need to be well organized and cleanly designed. If no one in the organization is willing to tackle the task (or no one has the necessary expertise), consider outsourcing. You might find a designer who would be interested in donating a little time. If the designer creates a basic template, you can have someone handle the page maintenance inhouse.

Another option is to use a third party to create your fundraising affiliate site. A multitude of organizations have sprung up to provide simplified Web affiliate fundraising. These organizations include: GreaterGood.com (http://www.greatergood.com), iGive.com (http:// www.igive.com), Shop2Give (http://www.shop2give.com), give2schools (http://www.give2schools.com), Schoolpop (http:// www.schoolpop.com), and 4charity.com (http://www.4charity.com). Most of these firms are actually for-profit organizations that derive funding from affiliate revenues.

4charity.com is a notable exception. This volunteer-driven organization pledges 100 percent of their affiliate revenues through their site back to the charity. The effort began as a Stanford MBA school student project to raise money for the Special Olympics. Once the project ended, the site continued to draw a strong stream of traffic. After seeing the continued interest, the organizers launched 4charity.com in September

1998. 4charity.com has expanded at a steady pace, with membership growing at roughly 5 percent each week.

What does it take for a charity to run a winning affiliate fundraising effort with 4charity.com? "The charities that have been the most proactive about sending people to the site have by far been the most successful—and many of them are much smaller than our largest charities," explained Scott Dunlap of 4charity.com. "The best part about 4charity.com is that it takes very little effort to direct supporters to the site, and it becomes a continuous revenue stream for them."

A great deal of the early roster of charities were national or international, rather than local organizations. Over time, 4charity.com has added a good number of local charities. "We let the members decide by suggesting charities when they sign up, so it has grown equally in national and local charities," said Scott. "I suspect there will be more and more local charities as we go forward since they seem to have more zeal." Through the magic of the Web, this California-based grassroots organization can help your nonprofit affiliate fundraising efforts take flight.

JUST LOOKING FOR SAVINGS?

Ebates.com lets you reap the discounts of purchasing through your own affiliate links without the effort of building an affiliate Web site. This innovative Web site was launched by former San Mateo, California Deputy District Attorneys Paul Wasserman and Alessandro Isolani in the spring of 1999. Ebates.com lets you set up an account to effectively pay yourself the affiliate fees generated by the purchases you make through their affiliate links. This brilliant scheme delivers what merchants and shoppers crave. Merchants gain sales, while shoppers benefit from the discounts. The site also offers a multitier plan, so that members can earn a percentage of the affiliate fees generated by the folks they recruit into the Ebates system.

CHAPTER THREE

Search Engine Tuning

Once you've created your content, built a great Web site, carefully chosen your affiliate merchants and products, then peppered your site with appropriate affiliate links, one important element separates you from success: traffic. You need a constant flow of new blood running through your pages. Search engines and indexes are a primary means of transfusion.

When someone goes to a search engine and enters a term relevant to your site, you want your pages to be displayed at the top of the search results. Achieving a top ranking is not an easy task. It takes thorough research, methodical execution, and a healthy dollop of luck to achieve the best results. The good news is that it doesn't have to cost a dime to play the search engine game. While pay-for-play search engine rankings have begun to appear (more on this later in the chapter), they are still the exception, rather than the rule.

SOME MATTER, MOST DON'T

While there seems to be no end to the number of search engines and indexes, the truth is that the vast majority of these sites offer limited potential for traffic generation. Think about where you do your Web searching, then ask a few friends which search portals they use. You'll likely come up with a short list that include sites such as Yahoo!,

Infoseek, AltaVista, Lycos, Excite, HotBot, WebCrawler, and Northern Light. Your goal should be for your site to show up on each and every one of these places. But you can't just show up on the fifth page of results. Your site has to be well ranked and well represented to reap the rewards of targeted traffic.

The potential for traffic varies greatly, even among the top tier of search portals. The technology and database behind one search engine can extend to many other directories. For example:

- *Excite.* The Excite engine feeds WebCrawler (which Excite owns) and used to supply listings to the all-important AOL NetFind.
- *HotBot.* Uses the pervasive Inktomi search engine, whose technology fuels a string of sites including Yahoo!, Snap!, The Microsoft Network, GoTo.com, Canada.com, Answers (New Zealand), Foo (Japan), and RadarUOL (Brazil), among others.
- *The Meta Engines.* Super search sites like Dogpile and AskJeeves query a number of the major search engines to produce their results. An inquiry to AskJeeves, for example may pull up results from AltaVista, Excite, Infoseek, WebCrawler, and Yahoo!.
- *dmoz Open Directory Project.* A massive new index created by scores of volunteer editors, dmoz results can be found on a wide range of Web sites, including Netscape, HotBot, InfoSpace, Lycos, and AOL NetFind.

Note: With more than 12 million subscribers, America Online's search engine can deliver a huge number of potential visitors.

Stand Up and Be Counted!

You must register your site with each search engine or index for the site to appear in its listings. Registration is a free process. You can register individually with each search portal via their "Add URL" or "Add Site" page. Here are some of the most popular submission page URLs:

- *AltaVista.* http://www.altavista.com/av/content/addurl.htm
- *dmoz.* http://dmoz.org/add.htm
- *Excite.* http://www.excite.com/info/add_url
- *HotBot.* http://www.hotbot.com/addurl.asp

- *Infoseek.* http://infoseek.go.com/AddUrl?&pg=SubmitUrl.html
- *Lycos.* http://www.lycos.com/addasite.html
- *Northern Light.* http://www.northernlight.com/docs/regurl_help .html

A plethora of services automate the registration process for you. While some of these registration services are free, many charge a healthy fee. Be wary of the registration services that claim to submit your site to an exorbitant number of search engines and indexes. Although some services boast of submission to 500, 600, or even a thousand or more engines and indexes, those services are selling fool's gold. Only the top tier of search engines and indexes are worth the time it takes to register. Free link pages, like Uncle Danny's Gigantic Page O' Links, fail to generate a great amount of traffic. Some of these free link pages exist primarily to soak up the email addresses of unwary registrants. Register with these page submission services, and you won't see an increase in site traffic, but you'll likely see an increase in the amount of spam in your mailbox (coming from those free link pages). Take a close look at the list of sites *before* you plunk down your hard earned cash on a dubious submission service.

That having been said, a submission service can be a big time-saver when it comes time to submit (or resubmit) your site. SelfPromotion.com (www.selfpromotion.com) is one of the coolest I've found. The site offers a two-week free trial period to test out their services, and a year's worth of their services costs a measly $10. You'll find more than submission services; the site also offers good solid advice. If you plunk down that ten spot, you'll gain access to a number of search engine tools as well.

Send in the Spiders

Each search engine sends out its spider to catalog your pages at some point after you've submitted your registration. The spiders run on their own schedules and exhibit their own habits. It's a good idea to watch your server logs for their appearance. Some spiders, like AltaVista's Scooter, visit immediately. Other spiders take their time in making the rounds. I've seen results appear in AltaVista a day after submitting a page. And I've seen sites take nearly two months to show up in Excite.

Popular spiders include:

- *ArchitextSpider*—Excite
- *Scooter*—AltaVista
- *Slurp*—Inktomi

You can find a host of information about each spider at the Web Robots Pages (http://info.webcrawler.com/mak/projects/robots/robots.html).

The traffic for my little Do-It-Yourself Shed and Barn Building site (http://www.geekbooks.com/walden/d-i-y-sheds-n-barns.html), as shown in Figure 3-1, increased steadily from the site's inception through its lucky 13th week of operation, with the site's shed plan page hitting a high of 198 page views per day. AltaVista and InfoSeek were the first two search engines to spider and list the site. It took over a month to show up in the Inktomi-driven listings, but the site took a respectable leap in traffic when it appeared with a top ranking in Yahoo!'s Web Page Matches (provided by Inktomi).

The D-I-Y Shed and Barn site had a huge boost in traffic when it finally appeared in Excite and AOL NetFind, gaining nearly 100 visitors a day. This increased flow of traffic was short-lived, however, as Excite dropped the page after two short weeks, for reasons unknown. Falling from a number 3 listing on Excite to oblivion was a painful experience. Repeated emails to Excite's support group were answered, but with a less than satisfying response. Excite's friendly support crew couldn't pinpoint the exact reason for the page's disappearance, although they offered that it may have occurred because my server was down the last time their ArchitextSpider checked my site. I took this with a grain of salt, as I had seen their spider in my server logs *after* the page's disappearance. Other pages on my site continued to appear in Excite listings, not just my most popular Shed Plan page. You'll see visible proof of the drop in traffic in the next chapter.

That's the danger in relying on one engine to supply your site with most of its traffic: Your site can disappear without a trace from the listings, with the result being a monstrous drop in site traffic. When your site traffic is slashed, so too is your opportunity for affiliate revenues. It's essential that your site be well represented on all the major engines, so that you can weather any storm.

Let's take a look at how you can build pages for the best possible ranking.

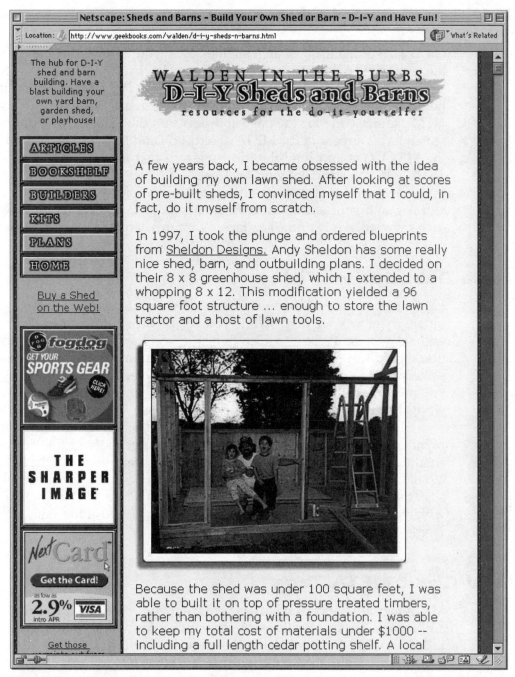

Figure 3-1 There comes a time in every guy's life when he has to build a shed. Well, maybe not.

GOING FOR THE GOLD

Go to each of the major search engines. Plug your keywords (and combinations of keywords) into the search box. Look at the highest-ranked sites. You'll find top ranking clues in the results. Pay close attention to how the page content and title reflect the search term. Open up the HTML source code for the page and peer into the HTML. How do the search terms appear in the META description and keyword tags? Study the META tags and how the most relevant text is used on the page. These help you structure your own pages.

You should strive to attain a top ten ranking for your most important pages. If your site appears on the first page of listings returned for each keyword, it is in prime territory to capture a targeted flow of visitors.

Use a Descriptive Title

Page titles are one of the most crucial elements in effective indexing. Ignore them at your peril! While you see plenty of page titles stuffed with keywords, it's best to keep things relevant and concise. The page title should read *as a title*, not solely as a collection of keywords. When someone sees your listing in the search engine results, the title should pop out, compelling them to click through. The mere inclusion of keywords in a page title is not a substitute for a well written phrase.

I like to think of Web page titles as the lead headline in a daily metropolitan newspaper. When you walk past the newsstand (the search engine listing), which headline reaches out and grabs you? Is it the lurid tabloid or the old gray lady? Keep page titles down to a manageable size; the search engines truncate long listings. Place your prime bait within the first seventy characters or so. If you add additional keywords, tack them onto the end of the title.

Build Great META Tags

META tags are optional HTML tags that sit within the HEAD section of a Web page. These tags allow you to include information about the page to help search engines catalog the page most effectively. Not all the search engines use the META information; some rely exclusively on the information contained in the page title and body, ignoring the information contained in the META tags. Of the many different kinds of META tags, only two are essential for top search result ranking:

- *Keywords.* These are the most important words and phrases found on the page.
- *Description.* This is a concise synopsis of the information contained on the page.

Here's an example of a title, keyword and description from one of my pages:

```
<HEAD>

<TITLE> D-I-Y Sheds and Barns—Plans, Blueprints—Build Your
Own Shed or Barn </TITLE>

<META NAME="keywords" CONTENT="sheds, barns, storage,
storage buildings, greenhouses, greenhouse, garage, workbench, work-
benches, garden, building, gardener, lawn and garden, residential stor-
age, tool shed, wood shed, toolshed, gardening shed, potting shed, yard
building, home storage, d-i-y project, post and beam, timber framing,
pole building, garden tools, playhouse, playhouses, barn, shed, storage
building, cabin, timber building, home and garden, do it yourself, do-it-
yourself, d-i-y, backyard, gardening, utility shed, garages, shed plan,
toolshed plan, barn plan, blueprint, manufactured shed, pre-cut lumber,
blueprints, garages, woodshed">

<META NAME="description" CONTENT="The hub for D-I-Y shed
and barn building. Check out our resources for barn, shed, and play-
house blueprints, plans, kits, hardware, builders, books, and articles.">

</HEAD>
```

The keywords should be highly relevant to the text on the page. Include different combinations of keywords, including misspellings and pluralizations, but avoid needless repetition, as it can hurt the page's search engine ranking. The spiders want to see nice clean tags, not a bunch of junk. They can turn their noses up at the slightest whiff of keyword spam.

Don't Register Your Pages Too Soon

Wait until you have a descriptive title, relevant content, and META tags on each of your pages before you register. Make sure that all of your pages are properly linked and uploaded. If the spider indexes the pages immediately—and it will happen with search engines like AltaVista and InfoSeek—you'll be disappointed when the spider throws the page on the bottom of the results.

Each Page Should Work on Its Own

Every page is a potential doorway into your Web site. Each page should be able to stand by itself. Spice the spider bait differently on each page to attract the broadest possible audience within your relevant topic. Don't run the same META tags on every page; fiddle with the keywords and descriptions to suit the content. Also tailor each page title.

Some spiders allow you to register individual pages. Other spiders want to crawl through and look at the entire domain for themselves, asking that you submit only your index (front door) page. Registering individual pages is a boon for highly time-sensitive pages. And it's a big help when optimizing rankings. If your pages are based on current events and happenings (or if you want to try to tweak your pages all the way to the top of the charts), you might use this technique. Just don't go overboard—you can be penalized for oversubmission.

Watch for Opportunities

Bulletin boards can present golden opportunities; there's at least one for every topic. When you look through the top-ranked search results on a keyword, keep an eye open for bulletin board message threads that are directly related to your site. Reply to relevant threads with a thoughtful, relevant message. Steer people to your site by including your URL and a clear, concise explanation of what your site offers. (Add something worthwhile to the discussion; don't just spam them with your URL. That's bad karma.) As people hit one of these bulletin board pages from a search engine link, there's a good chance they won't find the information they were looking for. If you have added an attractive and informative link to that page, they're likely to follow your link.

This technique won't generate a huge volume of traffic, but it's still worth the effort. It works especially well when you're having difficulty getting picked up by a specific search engine. Look for bulletin board pages that have been ranked highly by those difficult engines. Once you add your post(s), you gain the benefit of a great ranking by tapping into the flow of targeted information seekers.

Recycle Your Jetsam

If your Web site has been around for a few months, you may have some pages floating beneath the surface of your site. These pages may be indexed by the search engines, yet provide little benefit in the way of bait. To find these underutilized pages, pore over the server logs. Look through a month's worth of requests, searching for the spider hits. Once you find an underutilized page that's been indexed, turn it into a useful doorway page by placing relevant content (and attractive spider bait) on the page. Then sit back and wait for it to be crawled again. (This technique works best on engines that do not allow you to submit individual pages.)

Forget Frames

Framed Web site designs are notoriously poor search engine performers. The framed designs present a dilemma for most spiders: They cannot effectively crawl through the frames. If you're concerned with achieving the best search engine rankings, avoid using a framed layout for your site. If you are committed to a framed layout, use a search engine–friendly, nonframed doorway page as spider bait. And place really great META tags into the frameset, as well as some highly targeted and descriptive text into the frameset's NO FRAMES area.

Try Multiple Front Doors (or Sites!)

Your home doesn't have one way in. Your Web site shouldn't either. Each of the spiders has a slightly different diet. A page that ranks high on Infoseek, for example, may not rank as well on Excite. Find what each spider likes, then feed it. You can create multiple front doors or even complete sites, each tuned to a specific engine. Don't submit all the pages to all the engines. Instead, limit your submissions (don't submit duplicate pages to a single engine). If you don't, you risk being booted from the listings as a search engine spammer.

Get a Domain Name

Web sites that reside on free servers and community sites are at a disadvantage when it comes to search engine rankings, while sites with named domains have an advantage. Some spiders may be reluctant to crawl too deeply into a buried directory structure. If you're serious about your affiliate marketing efforts, the domain name registration and monthly hosting fees will present a negligible cost. It costs just $70 to register a domain name for a two-year period (www.networksolutions.com). While domain hosting can be had for between $10 and $20 per month. If you're really committed to the game, you can set up a virtual server account with Virtual Servers (http://www.vservers.com). These folks allow their customers to host a dozen or more named domains at one set price ($55 a month, as of this writing).

Consider placing your most important keyword in your domain name; as a result, you may rank higher in the search engine results, as well as with visitor retention.

Don't Play Games

Be responsible in your search engine efforts. Don't try to outwit the spiders. They're hip to the tricks. The major search engines often use technology to detect bogus META tags, repetitive text, invisible text, and domain spoofing, among other index-spamming techniques. If the search engine thinks that you're not playing by the rules, they'll kick your site out of their catalog. Don't run that risk; keep it on the up and up.

Be Patient, but Perseverant

It can take a long time for your pages to be indexed. Each spider works on its own schedule. Watch your server logs for their arrival.

WHAT ABOUT YAHOO!?

Yahoo! is different from the pure search engines in that it is a human-generated index, rather than a computer-generated directory. Actual human beings add sites to the Yahoo! index. Unfortunately, it can be very difficult to get listed. The Yahoo! index is intended more for commercial than personal sites. The bright side is that Yahoo! includes Web page matches generated via Inktomi. If you can get your site to the top of the Inktomi-driven charts, it should show well in Yahoo!'s Web page matches.

GET SOME POWER TOOLS

If you're really serious about achieving and maintaining top search engine listings, outfit yourself with information and software. The first stop should be Search Engine Watch (http://www. searchenginewatch. com); it's a free site, filled with lots of solid advice. If you're willing to plunk down some cash, two resources are well worth mentioning. The first offers a wealth of search engine knowledge. Planet Ocean Communications (http://searchengine-news.html) publishes *The Unfair Advantage Book on Winning the Search Engine Wars* as an electronic book. This book, which is updated on a monthly basis, provides an amazing array of search engine information, eclipsing what's available for free on Search Engine Watch. You learn all the tricks of the trade, and find out what works on which engine.

First Place Software's WebPosition GOLD (http://firstplacesoftware.com) is an amazing application that automates the process of search engine optimization, submission, and rank reporting. With WebPosition GOLD, you plug in your keywords, and work with the program to create optimized Web pages for each of the major search engines. Once you've built your pages, WebPosition GOLD submits the pages for you. After the pages have been indexed, you have the program run a "mission" to see how your site ranks for each of those keywords, on each of the major search engines. WebPosition GOLD queries the engines, while you just sit back and watch.

PAY TO PLAY

Don't have the time to fine-tune your pages for the search engines? If you have a marketing budget, you can buy your way to the top of certain search engine listings (but not all). GoTo.com was the first search engine to popularize the practice of keyword auctioning. The GoTo program allows you to bid on search keywords and terms, in one-penny increments, with prices starting at just a penny a click. (It's amazing how quickly some of the terms have been bid into the stratosphere!) AltaVista launched, then quickly shuttered, their Relevant Paid Links Program (http://www.altavista.com/av/content/paid-placement. html). For the little guy, Goto.com had the advantage. AltaVista's more exclusive program limited bidding to five-cent increments, with a twenty-five-cent minimum bid. RealNames (http://realnames.com) provides an additional avenue to purchase visibility.

START YOUR ENGINES!

As a kid, one of the dreams I entertained was that of becoming a top engine tuner, tweaking the powerplants of NASCAR stock cars or Indy 500 open-wheeled racecars. I knew I didn't have the reaction time or iron gut necessary to actually drive one of those incredibly powerful monsters, but I thought I might be able to turn a wrench. However, I didn't have the mechanical skills, either ... yet another childhood dream left unfulfilled. But now I tune my pages for the search engines.

CHAPTER FOUR

Keeping Track

Now your site is up and running. Traffic's flowing from other Web sites into your pages and through to your affiliate links. It's time to keep track of the page requests, click-throughs, and (with a little luck) sales! This chapter provides information on how to watch the statistics both on your Web server and at the merchant's end. Let's start with some of the basics of Webserver logs.

SAWING THROUGH THE SERVER LOGS

Bob Dylan first sang that "the answers are blowing in the wind" over thirty years ago. Forget the wind. Today's Webmaster knows that the answers are actually hiding in the server logs. But if you're like most folks, you're probably scratching your head right now, thinking, "The what? What's a server log?" The server log is a text file created by the Webserver software, containing a history of all the server's file requests. You can find an amazing amount of information in the server logs.

Poring over Web server logs isn't like reading tea leaves. There's no magic, no mystical secrets. Keep in mind that nothing is anonymous over the Web. Every file requested from a Webserver leaves a trace, in the form of a server log entry. Each file request carries information, including:

- *Requesting address*—either by IP address or named domain (if reverse domain lookup is enabled).

- *Date and time.*
- *File requested.*
- *Number of bytes transferred.*
- *Referring page*—where did they come from?
- *Browser*—including version and platform.

The two most important pieces of this data are the file request and referring page. These tell you which page was accessed and where the visitor came from. If the visitors came from a search engine, the referring page information can include the search terms. A single line (of what may look like gibberish) can tell you where visitors came from, what (search term) they were looking for, and where they landed on your site.

Here's a sample line from a server log:

```
rover.ski-week.com - - [30/Jun/1999:18:44:33 -0400] "GET /photo-
shopplug-ins.html HTTP/1.0" 200 58100 "http://www.altavista.com/cgi
bin/query?pg=q&kl=XX&stype=stext&q=%2Bphoto+%2Bshop+%2Bplug
+%2Bins" "Mozilla/4.6 [en] (Win95; U)"
```

Looking at the line, we can tell that the visitor was browsing from the ski-week.com domain (don't worry, it's actually me), on June 30, 1999, at 6:44 P.M. The visitor requested the photoshopplug-ins.html file, which totaled 58K. The hit was referred from a search on AltaVista for the term "photo shop plug ins." The visitor was using the Netscape Navigator (Mozilla) 4.6 Web browser on a Windows 95 computer.

That's just one line. Now think of *thousands* of request lines. The Webserver generates a line for each and every file request, including graphic files as well as HTML files. Your server may also keep a separate *referrer log*. Viewing the referrer log shows you only the referring and requested pages.

```
http://www.altavista.com/cgi-
bin/query?pg=q&kl=XX&stype=stext&q=%2Bphoto+%2Bshop+%2Bplug
+%2Bins -> /photoshopplug-ins.html
```

While it's not as bad as gazing into Pandora's box, you can go a little loony trying to make sense of the raw server logs. Using a log analysis tool is far more effective. A good log analyzer helps you to quickly gain insight into the traffic patterns on your Web site. If you are using a site hosting service, basic log analysis tools may be provided as part of your server package.

Here are five popular Webserver log analysis software applications at the affordable end of the spectrum. (Some log analysis tools can be quite expensive.) While I've included pricing, it's only as a general reference, since prices often change over time.

- *Analog*—Freeware!
  http://www.statslab.cam.ac.uk/~sret1/analog/
  Macintosh, Windows (3, 95, and NT), BeOS, and UNIX (various)
  (Macintosh version at:
  http://www.summary.net/soft/analog.html)
- *Summary*—$59
- *Summary Pro*—$249
  http://www.summary.net/
  Macintosh (including OS X), Windows, Linux, and Sun Sparc
- *Sawmill Lite*—$89
  Sawmill Pro—$199
  http://www.flowerfire.com/
  Macintosh, Windows (3, 95, and NT), BeOS, and UNIX (various)
- *Funnel Web*—$249
  Funnel Web Professional—$499
  http://www.activeconcepts.com/
  Macintosh and Windows (95/NT)
- *WebTrends Log Analyzer*—$399
  WebTrends Professional Suite—$599
  http://www.webtrends.com/
  Windows (95/NT)

If your Web site is hosted on a free site, you probably don't have access to the server logs. All is not lost. You can still use a Web-based site traffic analysis service to compile your server statistics. (Don't confuse these advanced tools with simple page counters.) The online site trackers work by inserting a snippet of JavaScript code into each of your Web pages. The code feeds the captured data back to the site tracker's Web site, where you can view the stats.

Here are a few online site analysis services:

- *Extreme Tracking* (http://www.extreme-dm.com/tracking/)
- *Site Meter* (http://www.sitemeter.com/)
- *SiteTracker* (http://www.sitetracker.com/)

Once you begin to analyze your server logs, you can tell what your visitors are looking for and where they came from. In a great number of cases, you'll find that your visitors are coming from the search engines. The referring URL from a search engine includes the search terms. If you use a good analysis tool, you'll be able to quantify the hits you are receiving from the search engines based on the specific search terms. This is very valuable. By studying the results in detail, you can ascertain the most frequently accessed keywords. You learn what folks are looking for when they find your site. And just as importantly, you may learn what crucial terms are missing.

Let's take a look at what a good Web site statistical analysis tool can provide. Figures 4-1 through 4-3 show a summary report of my domain (geekbooks.com) created by Summary. This report provides a good overview of what's happening on the site.

Every Web site has its slow and busy hours, as shown by Figure 4-4. The lulls usually occur in the middle of the night, with the traffic rising into the day. A huge amount of traffic on my site comes from corporate domains. John Q. Public wakes up on Monday morning, trips over the junk in the garage on his way to the car, stews over it in traffic, gets to work, fires up his Web browser, and goes searching for shed plans.

Weekly traffic characteristics show a rise in traffic into the middle of the week, with the valley occurring each weekend, as shown in Figure 4-5. John's not on the Internet on Saturday; he's out working in the yard. He starts looking for shed plans on Sunday, but doesn't get serious until he gets back to work.

Growth over time is easiest to see when viewed on a weekly basis, as demonstrated by Figure 4-6. Compare this to the daily bar chart shown in Figure 4-1. Internet traffic is influenced by seasonal swings and holiday dips. If they're on vacation or out of the office, they're not on the Net.

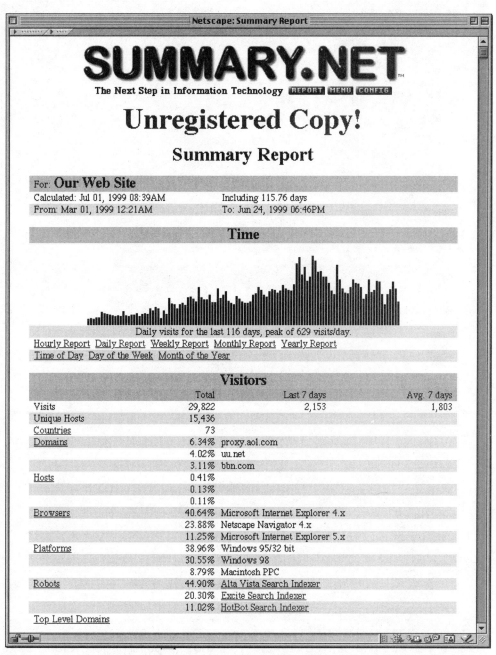

Figure 4-1 The bar chart demonstrates steady, then dramatic growth, followed by a significant decline—the result of being indexed and subsequently dropped by Excite.

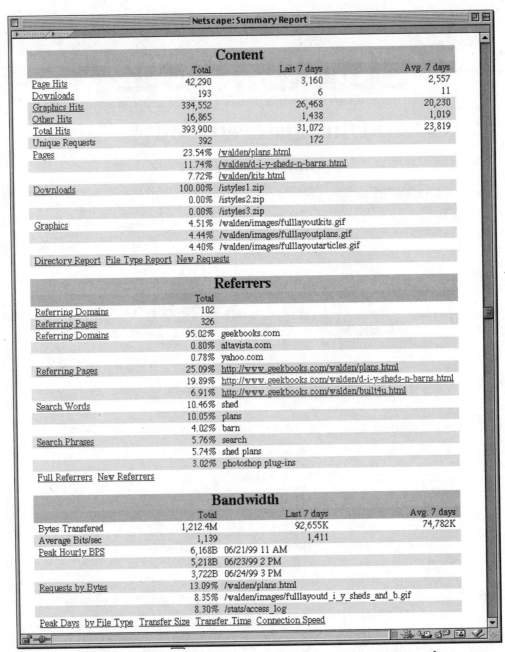

| Netscape: Summary Report | | | |

Content

	Total	Last 7 days	Avg. 7 days
Page Hits	42,290	3,160	2,557
Downloads	193	6	11
Graphics Hits	334,552	26,468	20,230
Other Hits	16,865	1,438	1,019
Total Hits	393,900	31,072	23,819
Unique Requests	392	172	
Pages	23.54% /walden/plans.html		
	11.74% /walden/d-i-y-sheds-n-barns.html		
	7.72% /walden/kits.html		
Downloads	100.00% /istyles1.zip		
	0.00% /istyles2.zip		
	0.00% /istyles3.zip		
Graphics	4.51% /walden/images/fulllayoutkits.gif		
	4.44% /walden/images/fulllayoutplans.gif		
	4.40% /walden/images/fulllayoutarticles.gif		

Directory Report File Type Report New Requests

Referrers

	Total		
Referring Domains	102		
Referring Pages	326		
Referring Domains	95.02% geekbooks.com		
	0.80% altavista.com		
	0.78% yahoo.com		
Referring Pages	25.09% http://www.geekbooks.com/walden/plans.html		
	19.89% http://www.geekbooks.com/walden/d-i-y-sheds-n-barns.html		
	6.91% http://www.geekbooks.com/walden/built4u.html		
Search Words	10.46% shed		
	10.05% plans		
	4.02% barn		
Search Phrases	5.76% search		
	5.74% shed plans		
	3.02% photoshop plug-ins		

Full Referrers New Referrers

Bandwidth

	Total	Last 7 days	Avg. 7 days
Bytes Transfered	1,212.4M	92,655K	74,782K
Average Bits/sec	1,139	1,411	
Peak Hourly BPS	6,168B 06/21/99 11 AM		
	5,218B 06/23/99 2 PM		
	3,722B 06/24/99 3 PM		
Requests by Bytes	13.09% /walden/plans.html		
	8.35% /walden/images/fulllayoutd_i_y_sheds_and_b.gif		
	8.30% /stats/access_log		

Peak Days by File Type Transfer Size Transfer Time Connection Speed

Figure 4-2 At a glance, you can see your most popular pages, referrers, and the bandwidth consumed.

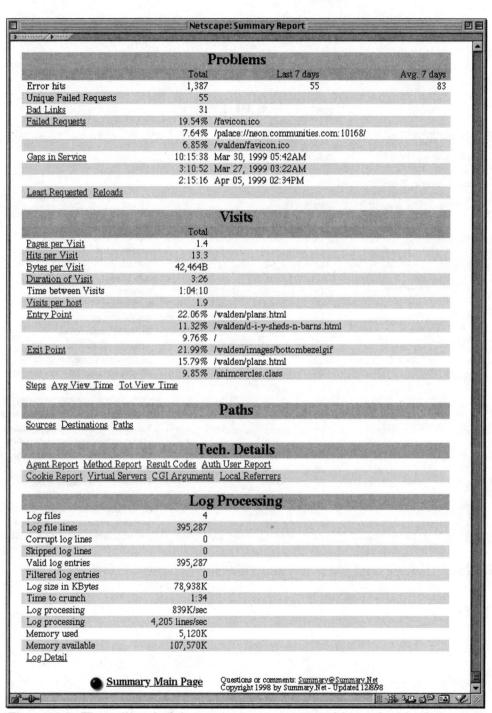

Figure 4-3 The tail end of the summary report provides valuable data on visits.

Time of Day

For: **Our Web Site**						

Calculated: Jul 01, 1999 08:39AM Including 115.76 days
From: Mar 01, 1999 12:21AM To: Jun 24, 1999 06:46PM
Displaying items 1-24 of 24 by hour.

Time of Day	Pages	Hits	Errors	KBytes	Unique Hosts	Visits	Pages
Midnight	1,433	13,117	19	37,977K	1,022	1,026	
1 AM	1,077	9,954	20	29,863K	804	810	
2 AM	911	7,809	13	26,125K	571	579	
3 AM	674	5,755	12	20,410K	426	431	
4 AM	673	5,350	17	20,494K	465	470	
5 AM	577	4,559	11	16,413K	436	438	
6 AM	811	6,131	66	22,290K	443	447	
7 AM	1,009	9,193	51	29,709K	721	729	
8 AM	1,539	13,217	66	43,551K	928	938	
9 AM	1,963	18,132	80	61,696K	1,353	1,366	
10 AM	1,943	19,793	102	55,176K	1,271	1,281	
11 AM	2,297	22,227	45	67,233K	1,528	1,537	
Noon	2,178	21,699	57	67,500K	1,420	1,433	
1 PM	2,469	23,802	37	72,131K	1,557	1,563	
2 PM	2,573	24,539	62	76,999K	1,732	1,750	
3 PM	2,488	23,747	56	70,594K	1,684	1,693	
4 PM	2,469	22,599	53	74,176K	1,722	1,737	
5 PM	2,285	21,481	50	72,910K	1,640	1,657	
6 PM	2,034	18,900	84	60,738K	1,465	1,476	
7 PM	1,961	18,329	45	60,411K	1,538	1,558	
8 PM	2,184	19,533	62	63,900K	1,620	1,652	
9 PM	2,536	23,862	62	70,087K	1,933	1,947	
10 PM	2,272	22,328	181	61,685K	1,752	1,769	
11 PM	1,934	17,844	136	54,610K	1,522	1,535	

Figure 4-4 The working day provides the bulk of the traffic at geekbooks.com.

Day of the Week

For: **Our Web Site**

Calculated: Jul 01, 1999 08:39AM   Including 115.76 days

From: Mar 01, 1999 12:21AM   To: Jun 24, 1999 06:46PM

Displaying items 1-7 of 7 by day.

Day of the Week	Pages	Hits	Errors	MBytes	Unique Hosts	Visits	Pages
Sunday	5,578	50,773	144	143.66M	3,375	4,220	
Monday	6,232	61,477	334	182.09M	3,646	4,314	
Tuesday	7,039	66,744	194	204.62M	4,018	4,788	
Wednesday	6,882	63,849	158	197.84M	4,130	4,799	
Thursday	6,479	58,245	191	187.35M	3,841	4,442	
Friday	5,616	51,208	119	164.78M	3,333	3,820	
Saturday	4,464	41,604	247	127.34M	2,877	3,439	

Figure 4-5 By Tuesday, they're frantic to find that shed plan.

Weekly Report

For: **Our Web Site**

Calculated: Jul 01, 1999 08:39AM   Including 115.76 days

From: Mar 01, 1999 12:21AM   To: Jun 24, 1999 06:46PM

Displaying items 1-17 of 17 by date.

Week Starting	Pages	Hits	Errors	MBytes	Unique Hosts	Visits	Pages
02/28/99	853	7,147	20	30.66M	374	457	
03/07/99	1,111	9,195	33	36.62M	481	668	
03/14/99	1,130	8,765	162	41.85M	501	694	
03/21/99	1,588	10,763	52	49.54M	778	920	
03/28/99	1,602	12,922	159	47.53M	927	1,090	
04/04/99	2,303	20,718	122	65.15M	1,154	1,559	
04/11/99	2,494	22,267	56	65.73M	1,202	1,781	
04/18/99	2,697	24,383	81	74.66M	1,315	1,793	
04/25/99	2,457	22,782	83	70.29M	1,247	1,635	
05/02/99	2,927	28,311	77	83.47M	1,421	2,154	
05/09/99	3,232	30,155	92	93.21M	1,459	2,283	
05/16/99	4,164	41,296	88	112.65M	1,881	3,397	
05/23/99	3,964	40,271	75	103.02M	1,759	3,170	
05/30/99	2,687	25,914	73	75.39M	1,294	1,911	
06/06/99	3,309	33,440	84	93.06M	1,564	2,416	
06/13/99	3,512	33,002	88	100.12M	1,542	2,329	
06/20/99	2,260	22,569	42	64.73M	1,191	1,565	

Figure 4-6 The week of 5/30/99 shows the double whammy of the Memorial Day weekend and the departure from the Excite listings. (This server log was processed during the week of 6/20/99. The access for that week is understated.)

The Search Phrases report, as shown in Figure 4-7, is an eye-opener. It enables you to immediately assess the popularity of each search phrase. What are they after? Once you know what they're looking for, you can fine-tune your existing pages to make them even more attractive in the search engine listings. And you can also plan additional targeted pages.

The Visit Entry Point report provides a listing of the first page the visitor requested from the Webserver. Most often, this is the page listed in the search engine. After viewing this report, along with the Search Phrase report, you should have a better understanding of what your visitors are looking for and where they're landing.

The Web Robots report lets you know which spiders came to crawl your site, how many pages they indexed, and the date of their latest visit. Take a look at the differences in activity among the most popular spiders.

If you're serious about maximizing your Web site traffic, you'll do well to study your server logs. But don't stare yourself silly looking at the raw logs. Get a good statistical package. You'll save tons of time and be far more effective. While you can't beat the freeware price of Analog, Summary and Sawmill offer a lot of bang for the buck.

TRACKING AFFILIATE SALES

While the beginning part of this chapter covered what's happening on your server, this section touches on what's happening at the merchant's (or service provider's) site. One of the key differences among affiliate programs is the reporting methods used to track traffic and sales. Without detailed information, you're operating in the dark; you lack the tools you need to optimize your site's effectiveness. A good system should be able to break down your impressions, click-throughs, and sales on a daily basis. A great system should provide detailed sales information, along with click-to-impression and click-to-sales conversion ratios.

The affiliate service bureaus provide systems that allow you to drill down into your information. Be Free and LinkShare achieve high marks for their reporting. LinkShare's system consolidates reporting for multiple merchants. Be Free's system, on the other hand, is structured by merchant; switching from one merchant report to the next takes a few more clicks. LinkShare's system provides sales and activity, geographic, individual item report, link type, net orders, product success, program level, quantity/price, revenue, and top ten reports. Depending

Search Phrases

For: **Our Web Site**		
Calculated: Jul 01, 1999 08:39AM Including 115.76 days		
From: Mar 01, 1999 12:21AM To: Jun 24, 1999 06:46PM		
Displaying items 1-60 of 3456 by hits.		
Phrase	**% of Hits**	**Hits**
search	5.76%	571
shed plans	5.74%	569
photoshop plug-ins	3.02%	299
barn plans	2.39%	237
pagemill	1.84%	182
adobe pagemill	1.51%	150
free shed plans	1.32%	131
imagestyler	1.25%	124
garden shed plans	1.03%	102
barn building	0.90%	89
storage shed plans	0.89%	88
plans	0.87%	86
photoshop plug ins	0.73%	72
yes	0.71%	70
shed kits	0.65%	64
shed blueprints	0.60%	59
shed plan	0.59%	58
storage shed	0.57%	56
0-	0.52%	52
building a shed	0.51%	51
shed designs	0.49%	49
barn building plans	0.44%	44
adobe imagestyler	0.44%	44
barns	0.41%	41
shed	0.40%	40
barn plan	0.38%	38
storage sheds	0.38%	38
barn kits	0.38%	38
photoshop plug-in	0.35%	35
squizz	0.35%	35
us1	0.35%	35
tool shed plans	0.34%	34
garden sheds	0.33%	33

Figure 4-7 The majority of folks came to my site looking for shed and barn information. Geekbooks have taken a back seat.

Visit Entry Point

For: Our Web Site

Calculated: Jul 01, 1999 08:39AM   Including 115.76 days
From: Mar 01, 1999 12:21AM   To: Jun 24, 1999 06:46PM
Displaying items 1-60 of 161 by enters.

% of Enters	Enters	Exits	1 Page Visits	Hits	View Time	Avg. Steps	File
22.06%	3,492	3,497	1,004	8,962	1:57	2.6	/walden/plans.html
11.32%	1,791	875	472	4,404	38 secs	2.1	/walden/d-i-y-sheds-n-barns.html
9.76%	1,544	965	746	2,607	1:27	1.7	/
5.57%	882	275	173	1,302	37 secs	1.7	/walden/barnsplash.html
5.52%	874	505	253	1,502	55 secs	2.2	/walden/built4u.html
4.29%	679	968	651	1,779	1:22	1.8	/biglist.html
3.99%	632	1,560	817	2,641	1:56	1.8	/photoshopplug-ins.html
2.83%	448	390	171	937	1:05	3.0	/walden/bookshelf.html
2.83%	448	1,147	277	2,565	2:56	3.3	/walden/kits.html
2.62%	414	456	168	1,092	2:33	2.9	/walden/articles.html
2.45%	388	4,870	970	11,290	2:43	2.5	/walden/images/bottombezel.gif
2.34%	371	300	88	847	1:10	2.9	/pm3buzz.html
2.29%	363	147	73	554	34 secs	1.5	/istyler-depot.html
2.19%	347	241	234	453	1:09	1.0	/robots.txt
2.11%	334	281	73	1,070	43 secs	2.5	/isid.html
1.90%	301	122	76	504	41 secs	3.9	/textures/summr155.htm

Figure 4-8 The plans.html page pulled in a whopping 22.06 percent of all the visitors to my site, outdrawing the home page by better than 2:1.

on the merchant program, Be Free's system can include an array of reports, including sales, traffic, product activity, link success, top ten best sellers, merchandise type summary, revenue (detail and summary), and page link summary.

If you join a slew of affiliate programs, you may find yourself spending an inordinate amount of time looking up your stats in all those different places. As a former affiliate, Commission Junction's Lex Sisney was unsatisfied with the different reporting methods and payment schedules. "We designed Commission Junction to be a Web based service to give affiliates the tools and information they need to be successful," explained Lex. "One screen shows the performance of all of the affiliate's programs. This allows the affiliate to check the effectiveness of their links for each advertisement and program." The Commission Junction system is similar to LinkShare in that respect, although LinkShare's reporting is a good deal more extensive.

Web Robots

For: **Our Web Site**				
Calculated: Jul 01, 1999 08:39AM Including 115.76 days				
From: Mar 01, 1999 12:21AM To: Jun 24, 1999 06:46PM				
Displaying items 1-20 of 20 by visits.				
Description	Visits	Latest Hit	Hits	KBytes
Alta Vista Search Indexer	387	06/23/99	539	5,279.8K
Excite Search Indexer	175	06/23/99	188	1,749.0K
HotBot Search Indexer	95	06/24/99	227	2,402.5K
Echo Knowledge Managment	26	06/23/99	64	761.1K
The Internet Archive	26	06/16/99	46	919.8K
Lycos Search Indexer	24	06/20/99	58	396.3K
Fireball Express Suche, Search Indexer	23	06/17/99	23	3.8K
Infoseek Search Indexer	17	06/18/99	48	349.3K
Digimarc Image Watermark Scan	14	05/25/99	27	131.9K
EmailSiphon, Unknown	14	06/18/99	30	616.6K
WebCompass Personal Search Agent	14	06/17/99	22	442.7K
WiseWire Intelligent Agent	13	06/18/99	115	1,289.6K
The Informant Personal Search Agent	11	04/11/99	11	615.0K
Microsoft Internet Expolorer, Subscribe	9	05/24/99	62	504.0K
Northern Light Search Indexer	6	06/20/99	16	76.1K
Infoseek Ultraseek Search Indexer	4	06/20/99	22	349.7K
Big Brother Link Validator	1	03/24/99	1	0.0K
GetRight Download Assistant	1	06/14/99	34	590.6K
NetMechanic HTML and Link Validator	1	03/24/99	2	0.1K
QueryN Metasearch Page Validation	1	06/20/99	4	42.6K

Figure 4-9 Among all the benevolent spiders, you find a poisonous one. The EmailSiphon crawls the Web looking for email addresses to add to its spam coffers.

What Happened to That Sale?

Sales data can fall through the cracks. I know first hand—it's happened to me. After making a (substantial) purchase from a merchant on one of my test sites, I was shocked when the purchase failed to show up on my sales report the next day. I waited a few days to see if the sale would appear after the item shipped. It didn't appear. (It still hasn't.) I sent a friendly email inquiry to the merchant. They replied graciously, and we worked things out.

If you feel that your merchant (or their service provider) has missed a sale, you should contact their affiliate support group via email. Allow time for the sale to make its way through the system. Wait until after the product arrives before you send up the flare. If you've worked with the merchant in good faith, and the merchant hasn't come up with a solution, it's time to consider your program selection options.

AFFILIATE WEB RESOURCES

Affiliate marketing is a fast moving field. The players and programs seem to change on a weekly basis. If you're committed to staying on top of who's new and what's hot, take advantage of the abundance of resources on the Web. When I began to research this book in 1998, there were just a handful of great Web sites devoted to affiliate marketing. Over the next year, affiliate marketing sites seemed to pop up like dandelions in a spring lawn; there are now dozens of sites. Regardless of the volume of new sites, the originals remain among the best.

Adbility's Web Publishers' Guide

Adbility's Web Publishers' Guide (http://www.adbility.com), run by California-based consumer advocate/lawyer/Internet advertising consultant Mark Welsh, contains a host of resources for the affiliate Web site owner. His *Commission-Based Advertising: Affiliate, Associate & Partner Programs* directory provides an at-a-glance view of hundreds of programs. Mark had a reputation of not pulling punches, often labeling programs as "Not Recommended!" or "Scam!" He's backed away from the approach. The site continues to provide convenient jumplists for tracking, log analysis, banner ad serving, affiliate management software, and other affiliate sites. Mark maintained the popular Affiliate-L moderated mailing list until it went offline in August 1999.

Associate Programs Directory

Journalist Allan Gardyne runs the sprawling Associate Programs Directory (http://www.AssociatePrograms.com) Web site from his home in a small remote fishing village in Queensland, Australia. The site includes links to well over a thousand affiliate programs in its directory, providing brief descriptions and a community rating system.

Allan's widely circulated *Associate Programs* weekly newsletter is a convenient way to keep current on what's happening in the industry, while the discussion board is a great place to sit back, chew the fat, and watch the mud-slinging.

Refer-It

Refer-It (http://www.refer-it.com), which refers to itself as "The Search Engine That Pays," features a large merchant-supplied database of affiliate programs. Listings are assigned up to three stars, with program details including description, launch date, fee, and number of affiliates. (The listings can tend to be a bit dated.) Refer-It provides a top ten list, a bulletin board, numerous articles, a newsletter, as well as an affiliate program of its own. The site was founded by James Marciano in December 1997 and was acquired by internet.com in April 1999.

A WORD ON MULTILEVEL PROGRAMS

A growing number of affiliate programs operate as multilevel arrangements. These programs urge affiliates to recruit new affiliates by offering to pay the original affiliate a percentage of the revenues earned by the affiliates they recruit. These schemes are referred to as *two-tier* programs (when they involve just two levels of affiliates). Multilevel programs may be attractive for merchants looking to grow their affiliate networks quickly. Whether multilevel programs are ultimately successful for either the merchant or affiliate ultimately depends on the quality and productivity of the recruits.

You won't find many two-tier programs listed in this book's Top 100 Program Directory. If you're interested in researching two-tier opportunities, check out Rick Bier's 2-Tier Web site (http://www.2-tier.com) or Allan Gardyne's Associate Programs Directory (http://www.AssociatePrograms.com).

WHAT ABOUT TAXES?

It's prudent to declare your affiliate commission fees as income on your tax return. Affiliate program commission checks are income, plain and simple. Many affiliate programs require a tax number or social security number on their application forms. While you're making money, the merchant is keeping records. You should keep records too. Maintain records of all expenses related to your affiliate Web site. These expenses may include any site hosting and domain name registration fees. You may also be able to declare additional computer expenses. Every situation is different, however, and the best bet is to consult with your tax advisor.

DO YOUR HOMEWORK BEFORE YOU PICK UP THE TACKLE BOX

If you want to catch fish, you need to situate yourself on a stream where the fish are running. Does that mean you should look for a stream crowded with fish and fishermen? Not necessarily! Don't look for just the biggest, busiest river. Look for the purest source of fish. Decide what kind of fish you want to catch. Then grab the right lures and find the right stream to go fishing.

Keep the end game in mind. This is about click-through to the merchant's Web site and conversion to sales. You want the best possible sales prospects.

CHAPTER FIVE

Merchant Profiles

Affiliate marketing programs are at their best when there's a tight fit between the merchant and the affiliate. This chapter provides a look behind the curtains at some of the best merchant affiliate programs. These companies have been profiled to help you gain a deeper understanding of what goes into building an affiliate program so that you can match your site to the optimal merchants.

BABYCENTER—www.babycenter.com

BABYCENTER—www.babycenter.com

BabyCenter was born in November 1997 as an information resource center. It was initially conceived in early 1997 by Stanford classmates Matt Glickman and Mark Selcow. The idea for BabyCenter gestated as Matt and his wife, Susie, were planning for their first child. Matt immediately realized that the Internet was the perfect place to research baby matters.

The site matured rapidly. Community features, including bulletin boards and chat, were added in 1998. As the site grew, the revenue focus quickly moved from selling advertising banners into direct ecommerce, when the BabyCenter store opened its doors in October 1998, offering everything a baby could need, from toys and car seats through layettes and backpacks.

BabyCenter took the wraps off their affiliate program just two months later. The company initially planned on creating and administering the affiliate program inhouse. After exhaustive research, they decided to outsource the program to Be Free. "We knew that affiliate expectations would be high," said BabyCenter Marketing Associate Lara Hoyem. "Affiliates want specific reporting. We knew that we didn't have the programming resources available to deliver that with an inhouse program."

Within a few months, BabyCenter had over a thousand affiliates. The company is extremely selective about the affiliates it chooses. "Baby goods are not ubiquitous in the manner of books and CDs," explained Lara. "It's not just about putting in a link or banner ad. It's about content." The affiliate site must fit the BabyCenter model. When Lara screens affiliates, she looks first at the number of page views, then at the site title (checking for relevancy), before she looks at the site itself.

Generally speaking, BabyCenter may turn down an affiliate application on site review for three reasons:

- The site was not available or under construction.
- The site consisted solely of buttons and banners.
- The site demographic didn't fit BabyCenter's model.

The BabyCenter affiliate program is growing rapidly, for good reason. They offer a generous affiliate commission (currently 15 percent), with average sale totals of close to $50. As of March 1999, affiliates refer approximately 6 percent of the site traffic and produce 3 percent of sales. The company is on track to double-digit affiliate sales percentage by the end of 1999.

BabyCenter is well-recognized in the industry for its excellent content and design. It won back-to-back Webby awards in 1998 and 1999, in the Living and Home categories, respectively. As the babies got older, so did the content. BabyCenter expanded coverage to include kids up to the age of three. What started out in the would-be baby's room now employs over 100 people. (Matt and Susie's daughter Emma is now one year old.) In just a short time, the site has mushroomed to serve more than 12 million page views each month. The allure proved to be irresistible to Etoys.com, who acquired BabyCenter just prior to going public in May 1999. Who can say no to a baby?

BAREWALLS—www.barewalls.com

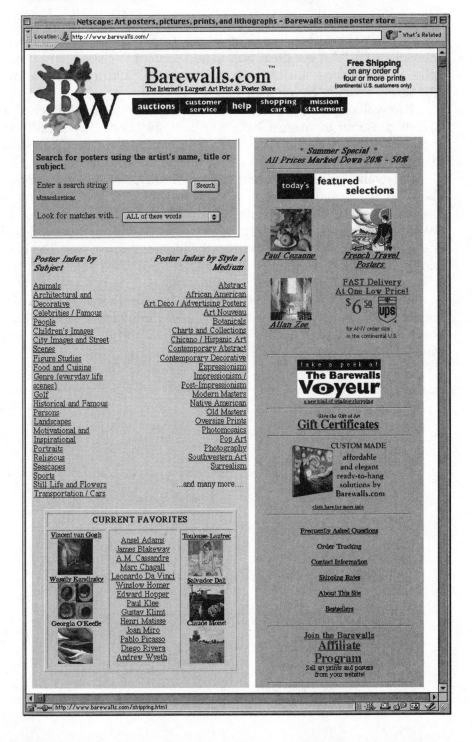

BAREWALLS—www.barewalls.com

Looking for a merchant that can improve the looks of your site while adding some coin to your coffers? Check into art merchant barewalls.com. "Art is a great way to add content to a site," said Daniel Spira, barewalls.com affiliate program manager. "Our program allows affiliates to visually enrich their pages."

Barewalls.com hit the Web in the summer of 1997 and launched its affiliate program in August 1998. The company reviews each affiliate application and stresses a specialized solution for each site. They strive to review each site within one or two days of the application.

Barewalls provides a wide variety of ways to link to their site. Their inhouse designed system allows affiliates to link to any page or function, including search boxes. "Our most successful affiliates are linking directly to specific products, as well as providing general links," said Daniel. Direct product links pay the highest referral fees. The company sees a 95/5 breakdown on affiliate returns. Five percent of their affiliates account for 95 percent of affiliate sales.

The company has worked hard to minimize their shipping costs. This is of direct benefit to the affiliate, as shipping costs are not commissionable. "We're happy to shell out money to our affiliates," said Daniel. "It's good for everyone!"

BAREWALLS—www.barewalls.com

Netscape: Art posters, pictures, prints, and lithographs - Barewalls online poster store

Location: http://www.barewalls.com/   What's Related

Barewalls.com™
The Internet's Largest Art Print & Poster Store

Free Shipping
on any order of
four or more prints
(continental U.S. customers only)

auctions | customer service | help | shopping cart | mission statement

Search for posters using the artist's name, title or subject.

Enter a search string: [   ] Search
advanced options

Look for matches with... [ALL of these words ▼]

* Summer Special *
All Prices Marked Down 20% - 50%

today's **featured selections**

Paul Cezanne

French Travel Posters

Allan Zee

**FAST Delivery
At One Low Price!**
$6 50 UPS
for ANY order size
in the continental U.S.

take a peek at
The Barewalls
Voyeur
a new kind of window shopping

Give the Gift of Art
Gift Certificates

CUSTOM MADE
affordable
and elegant
ready-to-hang
solutions by
Barewalls.com
click here for more info

Poster Index by Subject

Animals
Architectural and Decorative
Celebrities / Famous People
Children's Images
City Images and Street Scenes
Figure Studies
Food and Cuisine
Genre (everyday life scenes)
Golf
Historical and Famous Persons
Landscapes
Motivational and Inspirational
Portraits
Religious
Seascapes
Sports
Still Life and Flowers
Transportation / Cars

Poster Index by Style / Medium

Abstract
African American
Art Deco / Advertising Posters
Art Nouveau
Botanicals
Charts and Collections
Chicano / Hispanic Art
Contemporary Abstract
Contemporary Decorative
Expressionism
Impressionism / Post-Impressionism
Modern Masters
Native American
Old Masters
Oversize Prints
Photomosaics
Pop Art
Photography
Southwestern Art
Surrealism

...and many more....

Frequently Asked Questions

Order Tracking

Contact Information

Shipping Rates

About This Site

Bestsellers

Join the Barewalls
Affiliate
Program
Sell art prints and posters
from your website!

CURRENT FAVORITES

Vincent van Gogh

Ansel Adams
James Blakeway
A.M. Cassandre
Marc Chagall
Leonardo Da Vinci
Winslow Homer
Edward Hopper
Paul Klee
Gustav Klimt
Henri Matisse
Joan Miro
Pablo Picasso
Diego Rivera
Andrew Wyeth

Wassily Kandinsky

Georgia O'Keeffe

Toulouse-Lautrec

Salvador Dali

Claude Monet

http://www.barewalls.com/shipping.html

BAREWALLS—www.barewalls.com

Looking for a merchant that can improve the looks of your site while adding some coin to your coffers? Check into art merchant barewalls.com. "Art is a great way to add content to a site," said Daniel Spira, barewalls.com affiliate program manager. "Our program allows affiliates to visually enrich their pages."

Barewalls.com hit the Web in the summer of 1997 and launched its affiliate program in August 1998. The company reviews each affiliate application and stresses a specialized solution for each site. They strive to review each site within one or two days of the application.

Barewalls provides a wide variety of ways to link to their site. Their inhouse designed system allows affiliates to link to any page or function, including search boxes. "Our most successful affiliates are linking directly to specific products, as well as providing general links," said Daniel. Direct product links pay the highest referral fees. The company sees a 95/5 breakdown on affiliate returns. Five percent of their affiliates account for 95 percent of affiliate sales.

The company has worked hard to minimize their shipping costs. This is of direct benefit to the affiliate, as shipping costs are not commissionable. "We're happy to shell out money to our affiliates," said Daniel. "It's good for everyone!"

barnesandnoble.com—www.bn.com

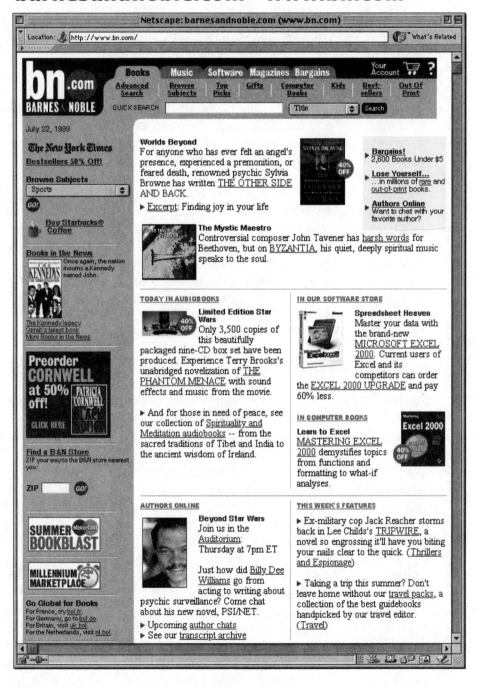

barnesandnoble.com—www.bn.com

Barnesandnoble.com has been a trail blazer in the affiliate space. Their site offers an extensive selection of books, music, videos, software, and magazines—providing a one-stop solution for some of the most popular goods sold over the Web. The company launched their affiliate program in August 1997, as Be Free's first client.

The barnesandnoble.com affiliate program offers some distinct advantages over Amazon's associate program. While barnesandnoble.com pays commission fees on every product, Amazon does not pay commission on out-of-print titles, used books, or gift certificates. Although Amazon offers a higher referral fee on direct hit sales, time has shown that visitors often fail to purchase the book promoted on an affiliate's site (instead using that book as an entry point to the bookseller's Web site). So that larger percentage is often a moot point. The barnesandnoble.com program is geared toward rewarding affiliates for each and every sale. Percentages range from 5 to 7 percent, depending on sales volume.

Getting started with barnesandnoble.com is an easy task. "We realized that affiliates need to get up and running very quickly," said Cherry Arnold, barnesandnoble.com's Affiliate Program Director. "Once they get into the tools area, our affiliates can build a store in just two clicks." The automatically generated bookstore creates an entire page full of links. Be Free's extensive online reporting system blows the doors off of Amazon's basic weekly email reports. "Thanks to Be Free, we have an amazing tool set," said Cherry. "In addition to being able to generate a myriad of links, our affiliates can slice and dice the sales information in their reports to better understand traffic patterns and learn what's working and what's not."

Affiliates have access to barnesandnoble.com's Auto Merchandiser, which provides dynamic content, along with special merchandising and cool offers. This allows for affiliates to take advantage of time-sensitive offers. "When the Starr Report hit, we were able to get the word out to our affiliate sites in less than two hours," said Cherry. Additionally, the company provides an amazing array of content and support. Affiliates have access to excerpts, selected chapters, and author chats. Support mechanisms include a monthly newsletter, along with traffic driving, HTML, and search engine tips on www.affiliate.net.

In May 1999, barnesandnoble.com went public, in one of the largest IPOs of all time. The company sold 25 million shares at $18 dollars, bringing in a whopping $450 million dollars. This remarkable war chest could slingshot barnesandnoble.com past Amazon in affiliate mind share and ultimately sales.

CDNOW—cdnow.com

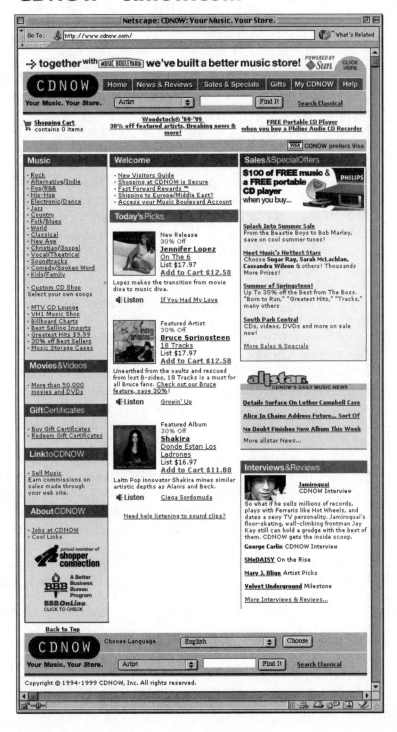

CDNOW—cdnow.com

With well over 200,000 affiliates, the CDNOW Cosmic Credit program is unquestionably one of the largest affiliate programs on the Web. The Cosmic Credit program is one of the very first affiliate programs, having launched in March 1997. It reached the 100,000-member milestone in September 1998, when CDNOW established relationships with GeoCities and Tripod. The Cosmic Credit program shifted into hyperdrive in March 1999, when CDNOW merged with Music Boulevard.

The Fort Washington, Pennsylvania company routinely offers special promotions and giveaways for Cosmic Credit affiliates. "We want to make this program as cool for our members as we would for ourselves, if we were members," said Deborah Kadetsky, CDNOW's Affiliate Program Marketing Manager. "Cosmic Credit takes a personalized, grass-roots approach. We love to give away autographed memorabilia and other cool stuff." As such, CDNOW has geared the Cosmic Credit program to the community, with tie-ins based on predetermined music preferences.

In the early days of the program, Deborah went looking for potential affiliate sites. These days, she has a steady stream of applications. CDNOW is relatively liberal with regard to their affiliate screening procedures. Sites do not have to be approved to participate, although CDNOW rejects sites with any illegal content. Nonetheless, CDNOW looks for really great music sites, not generic shopping sites. It takes more than just adding a banner ad to make a productive Cosmic Credit affiliate. Not surprisingly, the most successful sites are those that can boast a significant level of traffic.

CDNOW offers a respectable 7–15 percent commission scale on CD sales, with percentages tied to monthly sales revenue. The higher the sales volume, the higher the commission rate (as shown in the Top 100 Program Directory). The Cosmic Credit program was developed inhouse at CDNOW with proprietary technology. This gives the company a leg up when it's time to make a change. "When someone comes up with a creative idea for the program, we can implement it," said Deborah. That kind of responsiveness is just one indication of what's made the CDNOW program so successful.

ENEWS.COM (formerly ELECTRONIC NEWSSTAND)—www.enews.com

ENEWS.COM (formerly ELECTRONIC NEWSSTAND)—www.enews.com

As any day's collection of junk mail tells you, magazine subscriptions are big business. The acquisition of new subscribers is a primary objective for most publications. They must maintain and expand their subscriber base to justify the cost of their advertising: the more subscribers, the higher the advertising rates.

Enews.com has changed the subscription acquisition paradigm. The www.enews.com Web site offers free trial subscriptions for hundreds of magazines at the guaranteed lowest prices on the Web. The company debuted on the Internet as "The Electronic Newsstand" in 1993, initially offering articles and subscription opportunities for eight magazines. Over its first few years, Enews.com grew into a popular content site about the magazine world, using an advertising-supported revenue structure. It was not an easy row to hoe. After Brian Hecht took the helm as President and CEO in 1996, Enews.com changed directions and relaunched as a pureplay ecommerce site, selling magazine subscriptions in a content-rich environment.

"We saw that Web commerce was organizing by category," explains Brian. "And we found the company to be the primary player in its field." In the fall of 1997, Enews.com hooked up with barnesandnoble.com as the online booksellers' magazine subscription fulfillment arm. "We're the only third-party supplier that barnesandnoble.com uses," said Brian. "That says something. It takes a lot of trust." The company has also inked major portal deals with Yahoo!, Excite, Lycos, and WebCrawler.

Enews's official introduction to affiliate marketing was through Amazon.com's Associate program. After joining the program, they took a stab at building an affiliate program of their own, with a homegrown system. The program started slowly, with only a handful of applicants each day. Then they became acquainted with Be Free. "Initially, we were very wary of outsourcing our affiliate program," said Brian. "It was the first time we called upon a third-party company to run a core component of our site." The affiliate program growth was explosive. After joining the Be Free system, Enews.com was netting an average of 150 new affiliate sites each day. Today, Enews.com boasts a network of more than 20,000 affiliates and also has a special fundraising program for not-for-profit organizations.

"Affiliate marketing is the ultimate laissez faire business arrangement," says Brian. "There are so many points of indecision. You never know who is going to sell!"

ETOYS.COM—www.etoys.com

ETOYS.COM—www.etoys.com

The eToys.com affiliate program may not be one of the largest on the Web, but it's been one of the most successful. When the Santa Monica, California–based toy retailer's inhouse affiliate program launched in early 1998, it flew under the radar for its first half-year of existence. eToys began actively advertising the program in the third quarter, quickly growing their affiliate base from 600 to 4,000 affiliates before year-end. The affiliate program helped the company to achieve a very respectable $30 million in revenue in 1998.

With an introductory 25 percent commission fee, eToys quickly became the program of choice for child-oriented affiliates. In mid-1999, the company throttled back their commission schedule to a more sustainable model. "Affiliates drive many different kinds of customers to eToys. The most valuable, both to eToys and our affiliates, are first-time customers," said Michaela Bailey, eToys Affiliate Program Manager. "These customers expand our customer base, and we can assume they will purchase from eToys again and again. Thus, we are willing to pay Affiliates extra for first-time customers."

The intent of the revised commission structure is to share the profit on each repeat purchase, while adequately compensating the affiliate for new customer acquisition. Rather than a flat fee, eToys offers a volume-based sliding scale commission structure ranging from 5 to 12.5 percent. Affiliates are paid a $5 bonus for each new customer. While the move wasn't popular with all of the affiliate base, it was essential for eToys to look long term and institute a more equitable model.

The in-house eToys affiliate program team takes great care in screening all affiliate applications. "We visit every single one of our applicants' sites in person and make sure that their content is child-safe," explained Michaela. This ensures that only the right types of sites become eToys affiliates. As with so many other programs, the highest-producing eToys affiliates are those that go the distance to provide a value-added experience. "Our best affiliates are Webmasters who understand that they need to offer something special in order to make a sale," said Michaela. "The biggest success always comes from affiliates who find their own, original way of presenting and endorsing products they sell."

eToys promises to soar to great heights. The company sprung from Bill Gross' IdeaLab Internet business incubator and took flight in one of 1999's biggest moonshot IPOs. With a switch to a Be Free– administered affiliate program in June 1999, eToys is poised for orbit.

FOGDOG SPORTS—www.fogdog.com

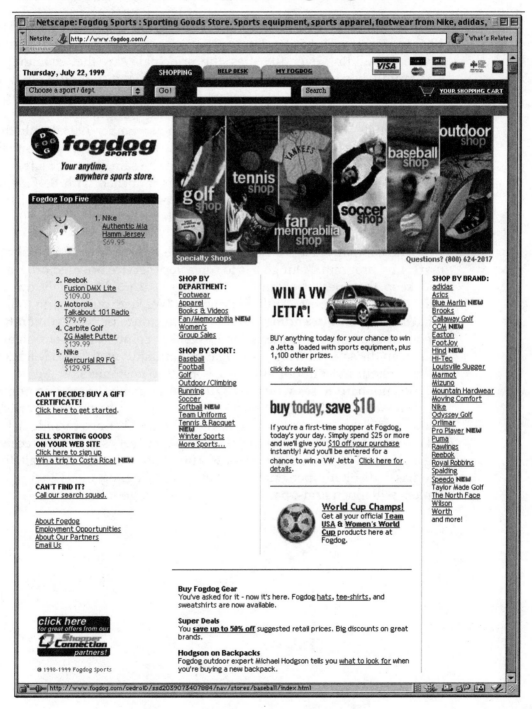

FOGDOG SPORTS—www.fogdog.com

The nucleus of San Jose, California-based Fogdog Sports was formed in 1995 to develop Web sites for sporting goods manufacturers. In the course of building over 100 sites, the principals saw that ecommerce was rapidly becoming the place to be. The company sold off their Web development business in 1998, raised their first round of venture capital, and went full force into Web retailing with SportSite.com.

SportSite was renamed Fogdog.com in November 1998. While the company had begun to grow its own affiliate program inhouse, they made the decision to outsource to Be Free at the same time the site was renamed. The Fogdog affiliate program was launched with Be Free in October 1998. With the help of Be Free's affiliate acquisition mechanisms, the Fogdog affiliate program grew rapidly to more than 50,000 members by June 1999.

The company takes a highly proactive approach to their affiliate marketing program. "Our goal is to run a very service oriented program and keep the lines of communication open," said Michael Feldman, Director, Fogdog Sports Affiliate Program. "We keep affiliates on top of what's going on by sending out a newsletter once or twice a month." Frequent promotions, contests, and excellent commission percentages help keep the sales flowing. "We treat our affiliates well," said Michael. "They are our most important salespeople and customers."

It's not hard to see why the Fogdog program has become so popular. The Web site fills a great niche, with a staggering array of sporting goods in a clean, easy-to-browse format. Product listings include helpful customer comments that make the shopper feel as if they're receiving a personal recommendation (or warning) on each item. All in all, the site has a distinctly personal feel. Better yet, Fogdog treats their customers with open arms, passing along plenty of goodies and sales.

FREESHOP—www.freeshop.com

FREESHOP—www.freeshop.com

Here's a program that can earn your site a nice return, without having to sell a single thing. Seattle, Washington-based FreeShop puts free trial offers in the hands of consumers. The offerings consist mostly of catalogs, magazines, email newsletters, product samples, and coupons. FreeShop pays their associates between 30 and 50 percent of the per-lead fees they receive from their retail, publishing, and manufacturing clients. The company also pay 3 cents per click-through, in addition to the per-lead fee.

FreeShop was originally part of Online Interactive, an early leader in the downloadable software market. The company has its roots in the online services. The Free Offer Store (the predecessor to FreeShop) was launched in 1994 on the Prodigy Network. FreeShop followed in 1995, first on America Online, then on the Microsoft Network. The Web version of FreeShop was launched in 1996. FreeShop has since abandoned the proprietary networks in favor of the Web. The company was spun off from Online Interactive in 1997, as the remainder of the company was acquired by Microwarehouse, a computer catalog retailer. FreeShop is venture funded, with a 20 percent stake held by Fingerhut.

The FreeShop Associate Program was launched in November 1998. With the assistance of LinkShare, the FreeShop program reached the 15,000-member milestone by the spring of 1999. The company screens affiliate applications, rejecting sites that fail to meet their standards. "A site full of links isn't a great candidate for FreeShop," said Sean Stewart, Communications Manager at FreeShop. "There's no reason for someone to visit that site—it won't send targeted traffic." The most productive FreeShop associates are those that are targeted at a particular category.

"We've found it important to keep an open line of communication with our associates," said Sean. "An email newsletter is a great way to keep them involved." To that end, FreeShop fills its newsletter with tips, hints, and case studies. While the company's core business is promoting free trial offers, they have branched out into ecommerce and sales.

FRIDGEDOOR—www.fridgedoor.com

FRIDGEDOOR—www.fridgedoor.com

Is your refrigerator door a hodge podge of ugly promotional magnets from real estate agents, pizzerias, and liquor stores? With fridgedoor.com, it doesn't have to be that way anymore. The Quincy, Massachusetts-based company's huge stock of refrigerator magnets is available only on the Internet.

Before launching fridgedoor.com in May 1997, owner Chris Gwynn was employed in a series of Webcentric roles with ZDNET, AT&T, industry.net, and the Yankee Group. The rapidly changing landscape caused Chris to endure five layoffs. The experience gave him a unique perspective on the world of ecommerce. With that experience, "I had a good idea of what works on the Web and what doesn't," explained Chris. "I started fridgedoor.com as a part-time business, with the intent to go full-time."

With a niche product, Chris knew that he had to find a guerrilla marketing technique. Conventional banner advertising was just too expensive for the bootstrapped startup. Affiliate marketing was part of the mix from the start. The fridgedoor.com Web site features links to their affiliate marketing program in the navigation bar at the bottom of each of the pages. But Fridgedoor doesn't rely on passively marketing their program. "We have one person on staff that looks for potential affiliate sites," explains Chris. "We look for small core groups of people that are really into a specific topic or character."

Being in the right place at the right time makes all the difference. "We've found that certain sites have a high conversion rate," said Chris. "Those sites often feature a very relevant link that goes right to a specific item." So if you think that the Simpson's Bio-Genetic Reconstruction Kits (Volumes 1 and 2!) are the coolest magnet sets you've ever seen, link right to those pages, rather than to the front door of the Web site.

Despite the small boutique feeling, fridgedoor.com generates respectable traffic and sales. "Twenty percent of our affiliate sites do eighty percent of our affiliate business," said Chris. To date, fridgedoor.com's busiest affiliate has been a South Park television show fan site. That affiliate site referred over 500 visitors per day (at the early peak of the South Park craze).

Advanced reporting was important to Chris. Affiliates can check their reports online. The site runs on Yahoo!'s store servers, which provide detailed reporting information. Each affiliate logs onto a unique URL to generate its reports.

INTERNET NEWS BUREAU—
www.newsbureau.com

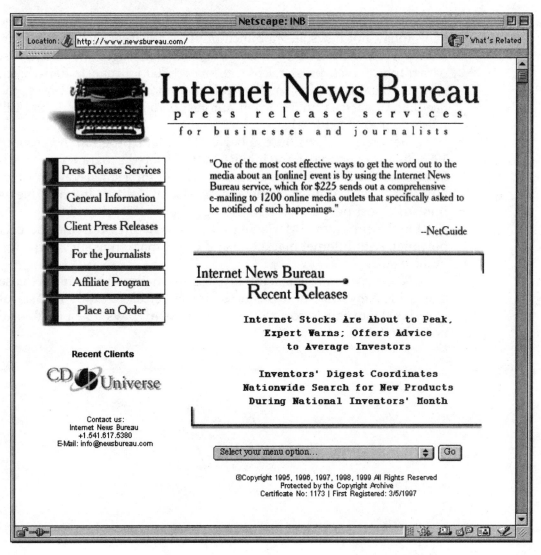

INTERNET NEWS BUREAU—
www.newsbureau.com

Need to get the word out? The Internet News Bureau sends out the news (okay, not news, just a bunch of press releases) each day to journalists worldwide. The company broadcasts its digest, with the first paragraph of each press release, to over 1,300 journalists daily. Each journal contains teasers for between five and ten press releases; the headline of each is linked to an autoresponder, which sends the full release out to the journalist.

The Internet News Bureau began its affiliate program in February 1998. In just over a year, the inhouse-administered program has grown to over 2,000 affiliates. "Our program pays off for a small core group of affiliates," said Annissa Anderson, Assistant Editor, Internet News Bureau. "Most people don't go through the trouble of qualifying their site for the program." Marketing-focused Web sites provide the best potential, with Internet marketing and direct marketing sites at the top of the heap.

INB services are substantially less expensive than press release giants PR Newswire and Businesswire. A release to the "A List" of over 1,300 journalists costs $225. The company pays a respectable 10 percent referral.

OUTPOST.COM (formerly CYBERIAN OUTPOST)—www.outpost.com

OUTPOST.COM (formerly CYBERIAN OUTPOST) —www.outpost.com

It begins as the quintessential high-tech start-up story. With just $28,000 in the bank, Darryl Peck launched his computer retail firm, Cyberian Outpost from his Connecticut garage in May 1995. Just four years later, the company employs 200 people at its Northwest Connecticut headquarters and Ohio warehouse. The Outpost has grown on the solid footings of its strong customer service and robust strategic partnerships, including its affiliate program.

There were just 200 affiliates when Alissa Perry joined Cyberian Outpost as the Manager of the Affiliate Network in March 1998. The company was already looking at outsourcing their affiliate program administration; in June, they switched to LinkShare. "Things really ramped up with LinkShare," said Alissa. "They assisted us in the process of building a substantial affiliate network." Within four months, the Outpost experienced an amazing growth rate of 2300 percent, landing 5,000 affiliate sites by October 1998. As of March 1999, the company had 28,000 affiliate sites, adding 10,000 affiliates in the month of March alone. The growth has continued at a torrid rate, with the Outpost hitting the 75,000 affiliate milestone in June 1999.

Cyberian Outpost chose LinkShare because they offered a turnkey opportunity to get immediate exposure. The Outpost wanted to build their program quickly. LinkShare presented them with an automated process for registration and link generation, as well as automated merchandising tools, including virtual storefronts. The LinkShare storefronts (pages) allow Outpost.com to instantly create pages by dropping products into templates. Each store can hold up to six products and comes complete with background graphics and headers. This allows the affiliate to create just one link to the page. Cyberian Outpost handles all the changes and updates.

Alissa explained the importance of creating a smart shopper with clear direction and a shopping list. "Our most successful affiliates provide a combination of content and linking to create an informed buyer. The person reading the page will be interested in finding out more, perhaps even purchasing the product," said Alissa. "The most effective pages drill right down to the specific product—they don't lose the visitor in the crowd at the front door."

The Outpost goes the extra mile for its affiliates. It has a team of four who have the responsibility to contact sites, to help fix broken links, and to provide marketing tips. Together with their weekly newsletter, the company works hard to make the most effective affiliate. With a strong international presence, as well as a distinct affinity for the Apple Macintosh, shipping products to over 230 countries worldwide is part of the game plan. Some of their most successful affiliate sites are in England, France, and Sweden. (See Palmstock.com, profiled in Chapter 6.) And while they are not authorized to export Apple products, the Outpost does a brisk business in Mac software and peripherals, with a strong Asian market share.

TAVOLO—www.tavolo.com

TAVOLO—www.tavolo.com

Tavolo (formerly Digital Chef) is a leading online retailer of specialty food, kitchenware, and other cooking-related products. The well designed and easy-to-navigate site offers an impressive and tasty selection of products, in addition to an extensive database of recipes and useful cooking content. Tavolo has an exclusive partnership with the Culinary Institute of America, the nation's leading center for culinary education, and recently acquired the assets to *Eating Well* magazine. Products, recipes, and content are interwoven in a superb manner. The site makes it easy to scale recipes, print grocery lists, save recipes online, and email recipes to friends and family.

Tavolo began developing their affiliate program in September 1998. The company did not advertise the program, relying instead on organic growth. The program has grown slowly to 1,400 affiliates as of April 1999. Tavolo plans on actively recruiting affiliate Web sites in the future. "To make an affiliate program a viable sales channel, you have to do some focused outreach," explained Chris Kane, Senior Director, Customer Acquisition.

Larger targeted Web sites send Tavolo the most traffic and provide the best conversion rates. Sites with cooking-theme core content work best. Individual chef's sites and sites with a great deal of recipes are some of the best producers. Tavolo screens affiliate applications with high standards. They're looking for highly targeted sites. "Our affiliate program is not a method to drive traffic," said Chris. "It's a method to drive orders." Like many other merchants, Tavolo has found that banner ads have proven to be the least effective method of linking, with contextual links the most effective.

While Tavolo began its affiliate program inhouse, they decided to outsource the operation. After a great deal of research, they company chose Be Free to handle the program.

VALUE AMERICA—www.valueamerica.com

VALUE AMERICA—www.valueamerica.com

Imagine what it would be like to walk into a fully stocked hi-tech department store. Now imagine that on the Web. You don't have to imagine! Value America presents the most comprehensive shopping environment on the Web today. The Charlottesville, Virginia-based retailer offers a huge array of products, in a Web site with an exceptionally clean layout and easy navigation. Its departments include apparel, books, computers, electronics, cameras, home furnishings, housewares, appliances, software, and sporting goods. Value America features name brand merchants across the board, with golfclubs from Tommy Armour, Titleist, and Callaway and appliances from Amana and General Electric. The merchant covers all the bases, with computers from Apple and IBM, and barbecue grills from Weber.

Value America launched their affiliate program in March 1999 with Be Free. Affiliates were actively recruited through GeoCities, Be Free, and through an internal affiliate outreach program. By the end of May, the program had attracted 30,000 affiliates, for good reason. The Value America affiliates program is extremely proactive, with an inhouse team that has grown from one to five people in just months, with plans to more than double in size again by the end of the year. The program's philosophy is sound. "Our goal is give our affiliates what they need, to be responsive, and to reward them," said Jennifer Johnson Lewis, Value America's Affiliate Program Manager. "If we do that, everybody will be happy!"

The company pumps up their affiliates in the same manner that a good sales director pumps up a sales force. Monthly affiliate contests and generous prizes—including a grand prize trip to Tahiti—help to inspire and excite the troops. In respect, Value America treats their affiliates as a true sales channel. The company allows—even encourages—affiliates to purchase goods through their own links. "We have people doing a wonderful thing for our company," said Jennifer. "We're very appreciative of our affiliates." And they're also very responsive. After receiving affiliate feedback, the company switched from quarterly to monthly commission payments, with a lower payout level of just $25.

The program offers numerous advantages to the affiliate. There is wide range of ways to link to the site and a huge number of products to feature. Affiliates can create "Hot Buy," individual product, and general department links, as well as dynamic price-specific links. The store features top-quality product photographs that have been created digitally in their own studios. Affiliates don't get a typical manufacturer promotional photo; they get consistent quality that doesn't vary widely from image to image.

With a virtual cornucopia of products to choose from, Value America provides a Thanksgiving banquet for its affiliates. And maybe a trip to Tahiti to boot!

WEB CARDS—www.printing.com

WEB CARDS—www.printing.com

You might not think about the printing business as holding great potential for delivery over the Web. Too many variables are involved in a printing job—finished size, paper stock, ink colors, and special handling—to make it a great Web-based business. Plainfield, New Jersey-based Web Cards has come up with a winning strategy. The company produces postcard-sized reproductions of Web sites, working from browser screen shots. In the four years from the time that they wisely reserved the printing.com domain name, the company has grown to gross over a million dollars a year.

The Web Cards affiliate program has been a cornerstone of the company's continued success. "Our affiliate program is the singlemost thing that has allowed our business to grow this fast," said Joe Haedrich of Web Cards. The affiliate program started in July 1997. Through careful management, it has grown to 3,000 affiliate members, as of June 1999. "We receive 600 requests a month to join our affiliate program," said Joe. "Of those requests, we accept one out of three."

Web Cards pays their affiliates on both a per-lead and a commission basis. Each request for a printed sample generates a $1 referral fee. Sales result in a 10 percent commission. The majority of the affiliate payments generated are for leads, which works out well for Web Cards. They are seeing a lead-to-sale conversion rate of 10:1. "We have found that people really need to see the product before they order," said Joe. "A ten dollar investment in a sale makes good sense." In addition to directly increasing sales, the lead generation program has enabled the company to amass an impressive mailing list of over 30,000 interested parties.

The company has expanded its offerings to include full-color CD-ROM inserts and business cards, all printed on the same 12-point paper stock on the company's four-color printing press. With the help of a dynamic affiliate program, Web Cards has put a brand new face on the printing business.

CHAPTER SIX

Affiliate Success Stories

The affiliate marketing boom is real. There *are* people hauling in the cash from their affiliate Web sites. This chapter covers five sites that have had the vision and the perseverance to succeed. As you read through the profiles, you'll see common themes emerge, including a focus on community, content, and value. These folks have made it work. If you have a great idea and the willingness to see it through, you can too.

BOOKREPORTER— www.bookreporter.com

Bookreporter.com's Authors of the Century section profiles more than two dozen writers with the greatest impact over the last 100 years.

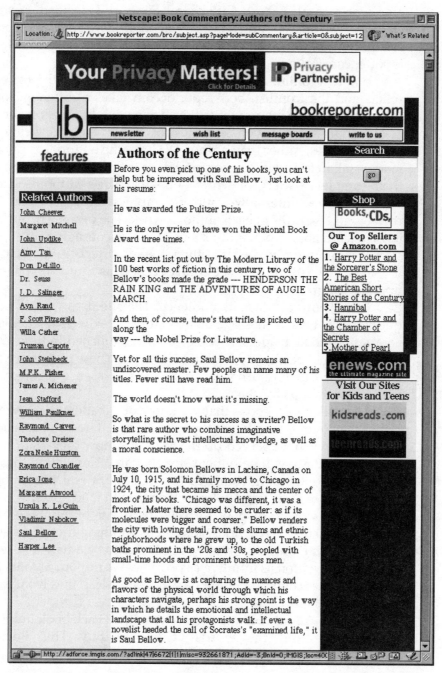

BOOKREPORTER—www.bookreporter.com

After spending more than seventeen years in the high-pressure magazine world in New York City, Carol Fitzgerald decided to stake her claim in cyberspace. Carol's influential book site, The Book Report, was established on America Online in August 1996. The Web site, bookreporter.com, followed in January 1999.

While the online bookstores are focused on selling the current bestsellers and the frontlist, bookreporter.com takes a different approach. "Our online sites are strongly author-driven, while Amazon and Barnes & Noble are book-driven," said Carol. "They are measuring performance by titles, rather than author. We have the editorial approach that readers fall in love with authors and once they do, they want to explore their complete battery of work." Bookreporter's authorcentric pages include articles, interviews, and biographies, in addition to links to reviews and excerpts of each author's work. The design encourages visitors to learn about each author's portfolio, encouraging multiple book sales. By grouping books by author, bookreporter.com facilitates backlist sales. The Authors of the Century section, as shown on page 97, is a popular feature.

Bookreporter knows its audience. The site uses weekly polls and questions, as well as message boards and a weekly newsletter, to foster connections to its readers. A book club area launched in June 1999 with chat, message boards, and instant messaging. These interactive features encourage frequent return visits to the site and a sense of community, as well as continuous feedback.

"We talk about books that we know our readers are interested in, rather than telling them what they should be interested in," said Carol. "Then once we have served up the titles we know they want, we share the ones we think will help them stretch a bit." Navigating through the site is a bit like winding your way through a cozy real world bookstore. The site uses a basic three-column layout with a 600-pixel width overall. This allows it to display correctly in all the browsers, on all platforms, at all screen resolutions. And there's nothing tricky to distract the visitor. "I never want to forget what it's like to be a newbie user, so we keep the navigation as intuitive as possible. We put our layouts through a five-second recognition test to be sure readers can find what they need quickly," explains Carol.

Links to Amazon.com are consistent, with each book linked with a cover image and the words "Click To Buy This Book From

Amazon.com." Clicking on a "buy this" link brings up the book's specific Amazon Web page in a separate browser window. The new browser window technique is crucial for maximizing affiliate revenues with Amazon. In short, the technique allows the visitor to remain on bookreporter.com while purchasing a book. If the shopper clicks on another link on the Bookreporter Web site and subsequently purchases that (second) book, both books are direct hits, each earning a 15 percent referral fee. (Indirect hits to Amazon.com pages earn only a 5 percent referral fee.) This is a key element in the site's success. "We partner the current book with the backlist," explained Carol. "Packaging books together on a page results in more book sales."

The site has been an Amazon Associate since June 1998. "Amazon makes it really easy," said Carol. "Their newsletter provides lots of ideas to improve the performance of your site. They have pages of Amazon graphics that can improve recognition and call-to-action for sales."

Bookreporter has two sister sites focused on younger readers—Kidreads.com and Teenreads.com—where titles based on popular culture mingle with the classics. "We see kids come into the site, drawn by whatever is happening right now," said Carol, "whether it's on television, in the movies, or in the news." Kidreads.com and Teenreads.com have a clever Wish List feature, allowing younger visitors—who may not have the ability to purchase books themselves—to click on a book and add it to their Wish List. Readers then can generate a handy email message for a parent or grandparent with each Wish List title hyperlinked to Amazon for easy purchase.

This same Wish List technology is also available on Bookreporter.com. "We tell our readers that by using our Wish Lists they can select the book titles that they want to receive as gifts. This ensures that they are not disappointed with their choices."

In all, bookreporter.com provides a great example of how a bookselling affiliate site can maximize their return. "You must have a point of view if you are a book site," said Carol. "We are not a bookstore. We are a book community site and an interactive book magazine. We tell readers why the books matter, not just what is out there for sale. We give them a reason to buy."

CHILDFUN—www.childfun.com

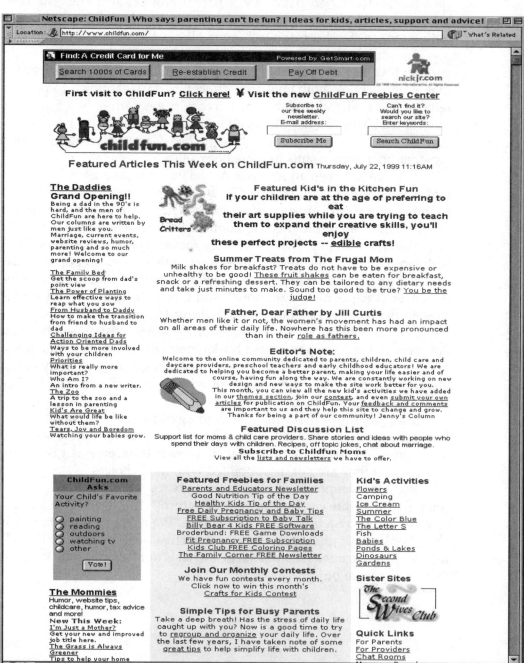

Everybody loves a freebie!

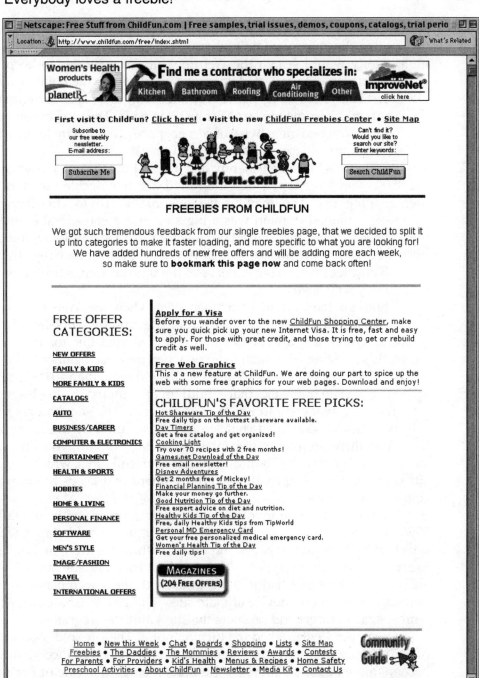

CHILDFUN—www.childfun.com

Jenny Wanderscheid was an at-home daycare provider and mother of three when she began building what was to become childfun.com. Each night, Jenny would search the Web looking for activities to keep her children busy. As she collected links, she would share them with friends via email. This led to Jenny's first Web site, "Tigger's Place." Eventually, the list of links became too large for just one page. Then the burgeoning site outgrew the two megabytes of server space provided by Jenny's ISP, spilling over into space on Geocities and FreeYellow.

As Tigger's Place grew, Jenny had a hard time finding a discussion list that covered the topics that interested her. She decided to start her own mailing list. The mailing list eventually led to childfun.com. Choosing a named domain was a big step and a considerable investment for something that started out just for fun. One day, Jenny told her husband, "I want my own domain." While the $100 domain registration and ISP host fees were a big expense at the time, as things turned out, it was money well spent.

ChildFun took off in December 1998 when the Web site joined Mom's Village, a grass roots collection of sites run by work-from-home mothers. "We're just a bunch of moms that started this for fun," said Jenny. "It's amazing what moms can do when they get together!" The site served over 150,000 page views in April 1999 to more than 40,000 unique visitors. With site traffic like that, ChildFun has entered the big leagues.

There's a real community at childfun.com. The site features message boards and scheduled chat sessions, in addition to the discussion lists. And there are plenty of contests too. Each month, you find new contests, with mothers submitting stories or useful hints, which become site content. All of this creates an environment that keeps those moms coming back for more.

Jenny first became involved with affiliate programs in the fall of 1998, with a distinct lack of success. "I thought I would slap a whole bunch of banners on my pages and make a whole bunch of money," she explained. "It didn't happen." The problem was that she started with affiliate programs that had nothing to do with the site content—a common tendency among novice affiliate sites. Things turned around when Jenny began to target and promote the site's affiliate programs.

December 1998 marked the turning point. The site sold $500 worth of merchandise through etoys.com that month. This convinced Jenny to become more aggressive. When she finds a bargain at one of her merchants, she passes the word along to her audience. "I really hunt down my merchants, looking for sales," said Jenny. "Then I give my readers a nudge in the right direction, promoting sales in the newsletter and with links in the sig file."

Through experience, ChildFun became an effective affiliate by offering items that moms want, including toys, parenting books, and free goodies. Jenny is constantly looking for new opportunities, but is careful not to get involved with too many programs. "You must find the right programs with things that your visitors will be interested in," she explained. "Then you must promote them."

It's extremely easy to jump from ChildFun to their affiliated merchants. The Web pages feature text links to the merchants in the site navigation bar, along with ad banners, buttons, and search boxes. While the links are abundant, they never overwhelm the page content. Video game and toy picks are linked directly to each product page. The site is not shy about mentioning that the links help with funding.

Freebies, like those shown on page 101, are among ChildFun's most popular features. The site offers a slew of freebie links, including postcards and graphics. It comes as no surprise that FreeShop is one of their most successful affiliate programs. Each time a visitor clicks through to FreeShop and takes advantage of a free catalog or merchandise request, ChildFun earns a bounty.

ChildFun stands as shining example of what can be done on a shoestring. Jenny works in the living room on her "little dinosaur" Macintosh Performa, in Claris HomePage and Color-It. (While she prefers working in a WYSIWYG environment for page building, Jenny admitted that "every once in a while, I do the text thing.") Her story proves that it doesn't take a round of venture capital and a roomful of state-of-the art hardware to become a successful affiliate.

"I'm just a housewife with three little kids in Minnesota, " said Jenny. "I did with my site what I wanted to see on other sites but I didn't see."

THE MONTERO-SPORT GARAGE— www.montero-sport.com

Targeted links deliver traffic to Web resources and affiliate programs alike.

THE MONTERO-SPORT GARAGE— www.montero-sport.com

A Web developer by trade (www.technocraft.com), Tony Schreiber built The Montero-Sport Garage because he had a difficult time finding information about his brand new Mitsubishi Montero-Sport online. Tony launched the Web site in February 1997, "pretty much the day I brought the truck home." An avid Mazda Miata owner and enthusiast, Tony was prompted to create The Montero-Sport Garage after his experience as a member of the Miata.net community. "I wanted to create the same resource that I had for my Miata," said Tony.

The Montero-Sport Garage filled a needed niche. There were no other Montero-Sport Web sites and very few Montero sites. Tony started with a small site, a mailing list, links to reviews, and a bit of content. As the site grew, Tony added a classified section and a message board. While the classifieds didn't take off, the message board proved to be the most heavily trafficked section, drawing nine times more hits than the front page of the site. The flow of traffic moved from the mailing list to the message board, effectively killing off the mailing list. This worked to the site's advantage as page views exploded.

With no competition, the site quickly grew in popularity, passing the 100,000-hit-per-month level in early 1998. The site now averages over 300,000 hits per month and roughly 600 unique visitors each day. What about competition?"If you can get in first with a good site, and no one can one up you, you'll stay on top," explained Tony. The Online Resources page, shown on page 105, provides links to news items, sales reports, and technical service bulletins.

The site does not participate in any banner exchange schemes. "I've never liked the content and look of the banner exchange advertisements," said Tony. "The site's not dying for traffic. I didn't want to tarnish the look of the site with ugly banners." He does include banner advertisements from ValueClick, however. ValueClick provides the site with brand name banners and a consistent flow of revenue.

CarPrices has proven to be the Montero-Sport Garage's most successful affiliate program. Tony signed up with CarPrices in June 1998. He added links directly to functions within the CarPrices site, including free insurance quotes and new car price quotes. Linking directly to the quote functions ensures that folks will not get lost at CarPrices' front door. Links were placed strategically throughout the site to dynamically updated pages where CarPrices provides pricing and rebate information. With this arrangement, Tony says, "I don't have to waste time hunting down rebates!"

The beauty of the CarPrices program is that it relies on lead generation, not on sales. Visitors are not asked to buy something on the spot; they only need to request a quote to generate a fee. The CarPrices program is extremely generous, with 50 percent of their lead fee paid to the affiliate. The Montero-Sport Garage has averaged a $600 quarterly commission, with their latest (and most successful) quarter pulling in $1,500—not exactly chump change for something that started out on a whim!

Together with his brother Joe, Tony continues to experiment with new sites and affiliate programs. Other sites include Honda.net, Digitacamera.com, and Technosite Exchange. Joe was the impetus for Honda.net; the site makes a valiant stab at consolidating the vast (yet unorganized) online Honda community. Digitacamera.com provides FAQs and scripts for digital cameras that use the Digita operating system, including the Kodak DC220, DC260, and DC265, as well as the Minolta Dimage 1500. Technosite Exchange (Tsx.org) provides much needed URL redirection, allowing users to change long URLs (like those from the free Web hosting services) into concise URLs like http://shortname.tsx.org/. With roughly 30,000 registered users, Technosite Exchange is poised for success.

PALMSTOCK—www.Palmstock.com

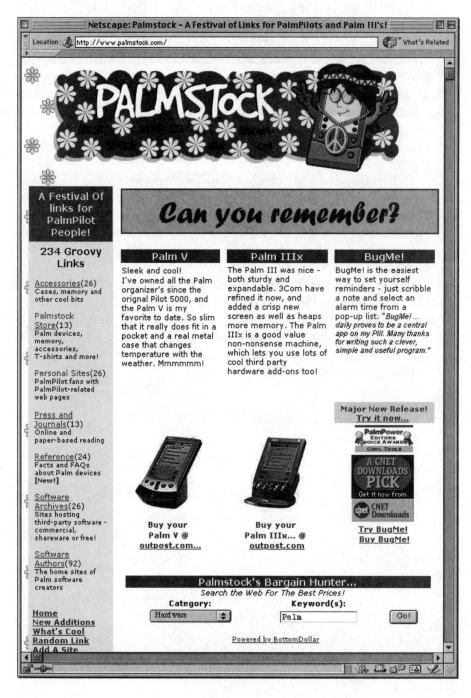

Look closely. There are carefully chosen affiliate programs among the other links.

PALMSTOCK—www.Palmstock.com

Iain Barclay's hobby of creating applications for the Palm III and Windows CE handheld computers led him to create Haus of Maus (hausofmaus.com) to distribute his shareware programs. Without the resources to purchase banner advertising, Iain needed a way to funnel potential customers to his site. He came up with RoadCoders.com, a Web site filled with content focused on software development for hand-held computers.

His foray into affiliate programs sprang from his first efforts with RoadCoders.com, when he signed up as an Amazon Associate to sell Windows CE programming books (there were no Palm III programming books at the time). Iain was looking for a way to sell the Metroworks software development environment, CodeWarrior. The folks at Metroworks suggested that Iain get in contact with Outpost.com, which at the time did not yet have its affiliate program in place. RoadCoders.com became one of the very first Outpost.com affiliates, primarily selling CodeWarrior and Palm Pilots.

After setting up RoadCoders, Iain was bitten by the bug. He launched two new content sites, palmIII.org and Palmstock.com, to drive more traffic to hausofmaus.com. Both of the sites were very successful Outpost affiliates. Over time, Iain sold the RoadCoders Web site to EarthWeb and shuttered the palmIII.org site (to avoid any potential copyright issues with 3Com). Palmstock.com remains, attracting hundreds of visitors each day, while it drives traffic to Haus of Maus.

All of Iain's sites basically run themselves. Users submit content in the form of links. Iain screens the links before they are posted. Because of his busy schedule, Iain doesn't have the opportunity to monitor the server logs and site traffic on a daily basis. However, Outpost.com's extensive reporting through the LinkShare network makes it easy to stay on top of affiliate traffic and sales. The Palmstock Store, as shown on page 109, provides links to many Palm resources.

The sites have attained impressive affiliate results. In March 1999, Palmstock.com delivered approximately 4,000 click-throughs to Outpost.com. With an average of over 100 visitors a day, Palmstock rang up 37 purchases. The familiar Outpost.com brand has helped Palmstock.com to achieve purchase rates ranging between 1 and 2 percent of their click-through rate.

Familiarity has also been a key to the success of the sites. People need to know you're out there, and a great name goes a long way.

"Having a fairly memorable domain name makes it easy for people to remember to come back to your site," said Iain. "Domain names are cheap. Making a new site is a minimal investment." Iain's Web host allows him to maintain several virtual domains with no increase in his monthly fees.

Iain's dabbled with a number of additional affiliate programs, including one for CD-ROMs, but he's found that a focused approach works best. Music CD-ROMs sold dismally. In addition to the Outpost.com program, he's achieved excellent results with BottomDollar.com comparative shopping referral program. In the December 1998 Christmas buying rush, the sites pulled down over $1,000 in revenues from the Bottom Dollar program.

RIVERSVILLE GARDEN SUPPLY—
www.riversville.com

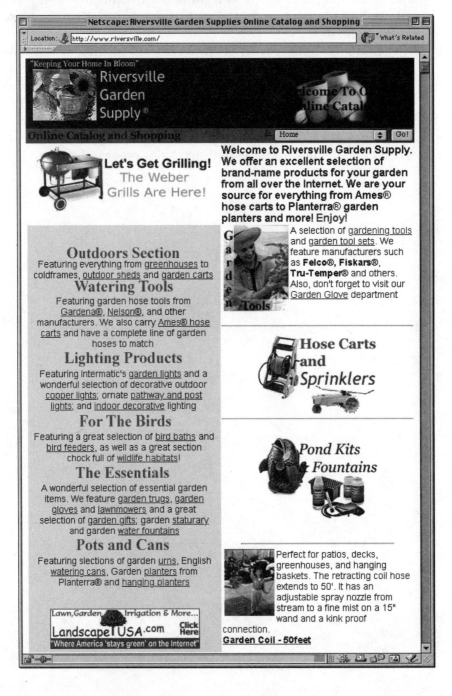

After all that planting and weeding, a gardener has to have a place to rest.

RIVERSVILLE GARDEN SUPPLY— www.riversville.com

Tony Lowenstein is a virtual shopkeeper in every sense of the term. His Web site, Riversville Garden Supply, is a full-service garden center that exists only on the Internet. Riversville is purely an affiliate play: The site has no warehouse, no storefront, no shipping department, and no employees. Nonetheless, Tony's customers frequent one of the most service-oriented and profitable commerce sites on the Web.

Riversville Garden Supply is an inspiration born of perspiration. Tony spent two months planning and researching the site. He designed it with the broadest possible appeal. "I built Riversville for the masses. I didn't bother with Java this and Java that," said Tony. "A complex site can bring an older computer down to its knees." Tony speaks from experience, as the entire site was built using Adobe PageMill 3 on a 75-mhz Macintosh Performa. The site use a clean design with percentage-based tables that resize to fit all monitor sizes. Table cell backgrounds are colored to create the page structure. Graphics are kept to a minimum, other than product shots. And that's where the beauty of the site shows.

The product is the content at Riversville. Everything drives to the sale. All links are to affiliate merchants, not to links that don't pay. Tony is very up-front in his role as an affiliate Web site, displaying identity buttons for his primary affiliate merchants: Value America, Etera, and Landscape USA. (Riversville also features affiliate links to Widerview Village, Superbuild, Brookstone, and Borders.) "If you tell people you are providing an affiliate service, you build trust with your customers," said Tony.

"How can I," Tony asked, "one person on a four-year-old Macintosh (that I share with my son's games) compete with the likes of Garden.com and Smith and Hawken?" The answer was in careful merchant selection. And Tony's biggest success has been with the Value America program. "It's a matter of trust," said Tony. That's why I've chosen Value America. Once they're at the order page, the customer has forgotten that they came from Riversville." When it comes time for consumers to pull out the credit card, they have to feel comfortable with the merchant.

Value America provides Riversville with a formidable number of product offerings and a high level of affiliate support. "Value America's picture quality is amazing," said Tony. "With other programs, I found myself asking, 'Is that a boot or a scarecrow?' Value America shoots a great deal of their own photography. They take the photos, clean them up in the studio, drop shadow them, and get them ready for the Web." Tony's also a big fan of Be Free's link generation system. "The Be Free interface is easy to use," said Tony. "I search for the product, make my code, then copy and paste it into PageMill's HTML source mode." This lets Tony concentrate on picking the right products, rather than spend his time dinking around in Photoshop or tangling with thorny linking.

Tony's learned to move his busiest sellers up to the front door of the site. "Move your hottest sellers up front," he explained. "Supermarkets have been doing the same thing for fifty years!" It's a true shopkeeper's approach often forgotten in today's world. Tony's found that people are looking for things on the Internet that they can't find at their local store. Each day brings confirmation in this theory, in dozens of emails message from customers searching for specific products. Inquiries come from around the world.

While there are plenty of great products at Riversville Garden Supply, there's one thing you *won't* find: advertising banners. The visual clutter of bannerization has been snubbed in favor of pure product links. The site does not participate in any banner exchange programs, instead relying solely on its search engine rankings and opt-in email list to drive traffic.

Persistence and attention to detail have paid off. After just a couple of months on the Web, Riversville has experienced an impressive amount of traffic and product sales. The site's results through the Value America program show this most clearly. As of early June 1999 the site was serving up an average of 700 unique domains each day, viewing 7,800 Value America product impressions. This generated an average of 1,000 click-throughs each day, with an average daily sales rate of $800. Click-through rates ranged between 15 and 22 percent, scoring an impressive 5 percent conversion to sale. Riversville offers the right products to the right people at the right time. And while June is prime time for the gardeners, Tony hopes to even out the seasonal dips with additional departments. The Outdoor Garden Chairs page, as shown on page 113, is a nice addition to the site.

When the project began, Tony thought to himself, "I'm going to give this a shot. If it's successful, that's great. If not, what have I lost?" With a solid footing in the virtual world and no concrete expenses, Riversville can do nothing but make a profit. As Tony is proud to say, "Remember, this is only costing me nine bucks a month for my host!"

GO MAKE IT HAPPEN

What's the difference between a successful affiliate site and an unsuccessful one? These flourishing sites should give you a clue. Each Webmaster started with an excellent concept. Each built a content-rich, community-centered site with affiliate links that give their visitors a compelling reason to click through and buy. These sites aren't crammed full of banners and buttons, nor are they mere shopping malls. They exist with a purpose. Take their lead. Turn your dream into reality. Virtually.

CHAPTER SEVEN

The Top 100 Directory

The companies included in the Top 100 Directory represent the cream of the crop—the best affiliate programs on the Web today. The directory focuses on better-known, well capitalized merchants. The selection and qualification process involved personal contact and polling of each of the companies. The directory doesn't seek to provide information on *all* the affiliate programs out there, just the programs that offer the broadest appeal. While the Web-based affiliate program directories offer greater numbers of programs, those sheer numbers can make the selection process tedious and time-consuming. The Top 100 Directory separates the wheat from the chaff.

You won't find any self-published books or marketing programs in the Top 100 Directory. While the books and programs offered by folks like Declan Dunn, Ken Evoy, Marlone Sanders, and others have been highly rated by Web-based affiliate directories, they sell to a select audience. These programs do not appeal to the widest range of Web sites. There is value in some of these programs when used on the right type of site, but they won't play for a PTA fundraising effort. You might want to read Declan's book, for example, *before* you plan your fundraiser, but you probably wouldn't offer the program to the moms and dads in your community. You'll do far better with children's books, toys, and clothing.

Year Affiliate Program Established

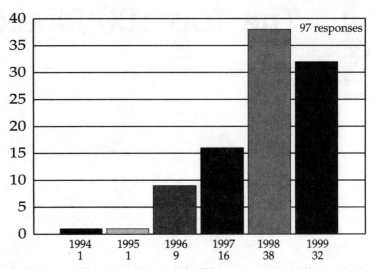

Figure 7-1 The popularity of affiliate programs is exploding. 1999 is poised to continue the upward trend.

AFFILIATE PROGRAM INDUSTRY STATISTICS

The collection of affiliate program data found in the Top 100 Directory provides a valuable glimpse at the industry. By tabulating the results, we gain insight into a number of key data points. The following section illustrates important statistics with simple charts. Affiliate marketing is clearly on the rise. Figure 7-1 demonstrates the strong growth in the number of affiliate programs, with the majority of Top 100 programs launching in 1998 and the first half of 1999.

Affiliate marketing efforts are getting larger, and many are reaching critical mass, as shown in Figure 7-2, with programs adding members at a rapid rate. The Amazon.com and CDNOW programs each boast over 200,000 members. Barnesandnoble.com has over 100,000 affiliates, as does Reel.com and the One and Only Network. The ranks between 50,000 and 100,000 include Outpost.com and Beyond.com.

A check in the mailbox is a great incentive. Most of the Top 100 programs understand this and pay their producers promptly. Figure 7-3 shows the split in payment schedules, while Figure 7.4 shows the minimum account balance eligible for payout. There's a trend towards smaller payout balances and monthly payments.

Number of Affiliates

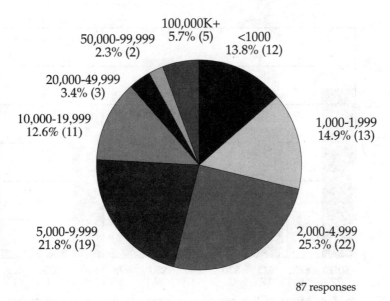

87 responses

Figure 7-2 Slightly more than half the Top 100 programs have fewer than 5,000 participants. This percentage should decrease rapidly.

Payment Schedule

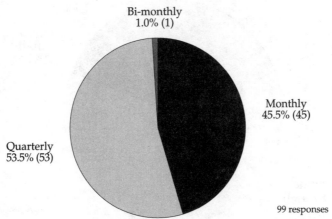

99 responses

Figure 7-3 Monthly payouts are more popular with affiliates.

Payment If Over

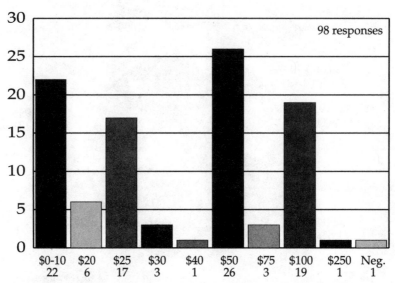

Figure 7-4 Most of the programs pay out when the account balance is $50 or less.

Type of Reporting

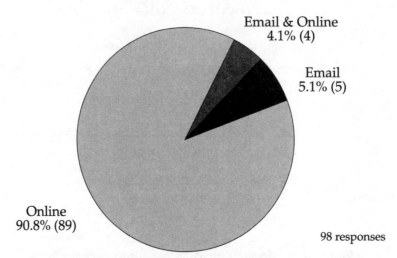

Figure 7-5 Email-only reporting is on the wane.

OK to Buy Through Link?

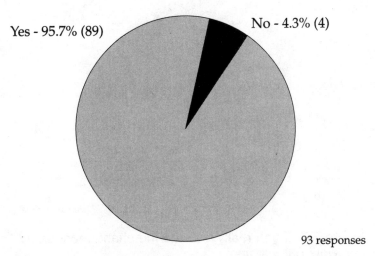

Yes - 95.7% (89)   No - 4.3% (4)

93 responses

Figure 7-6 Amazon is one of the handful of companies
that swim against the tide.

Affiliates want to see their statistics on a daily basis. Online reporting has quickly become the norm, as shown by Figure 7-5. The vast majority of programs offer online reporting, with a handful of programs offering both online and email reporting. Checking statistics on a daily basis can be crucial when implementing (and experimenting with) timely marketing campaigns.

The merchant/affiliate relationship is a key issue. When a merchant allows an affiliate to buy through their own links, it fosters a better relationship. As shown by Figure 7.6, an overwhelming majority of programs say, "Yes, it's okay to buy through your own links!" This practice can be thought of as being similar to an employee discount (although the affiliate is more akin to a contractor).

A good number of merchants want a monogamous relationship. Exclusivity is an issue with roughly one out of five programs, as shown by Figure 7-6.

So where are the geographic hot spots for ecommerce? It should come as no surprise that California trumps the rest of the states, as shown by Figure 7.8. Massachusetts, New York, New Jersey, Washington state, Virginia, Georgia, and the rest of the pack trail behind.

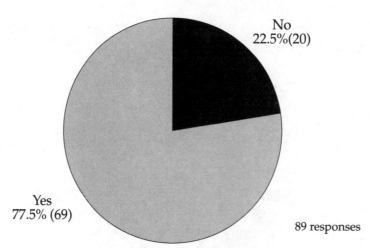

OK to Link to Competitors?

No
22.5%(20)

Yes
77.5% (69)

89 responses

Figure 7-7 If you really love the merchant, monogamy
can work out just fine.

Most Popular States

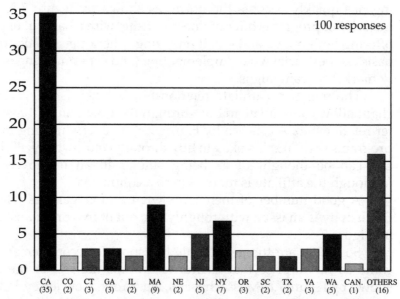

CA (35)	CO (2)	CT (3)	GA (3)	IL (2)	MA (9)	NE (2)	NJ (5)	NY (7)	OR (3)	SC (2)	TX (2)	VA (3)	WA (5)	CAN. (1)	OTHERS (16)

100 responses

Figure 7-8 Easy access to venture capital in San Francisco
and Silicon Valley puts California over the top.

Publicy Traded

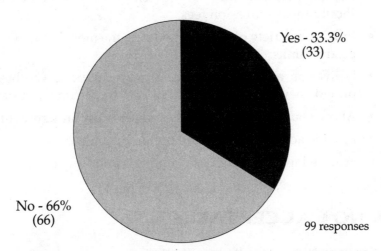

Yes - 33.3%
(33)

No - 66%
(66)

99 responses

Figure 7.9 Stock analysts would do well to look closely at the company's affiliate program when evaluating ecommerce IPOs.

Where's the next hot Internet IPO? As this manuscript was being written, a number of the Top 100 companies went public, including eToys, Autoweb, iTurf (Delia's), barnesandnoble.com, and NextCard. Figure 7.9 shows that there's potential for plenty of IPO action yet to come, with two-thirds of the Top 100 still privately held.

In many cases, companies were not able to divulge all the information requested. Privately held companies generally do not provide revenue information, although they deliver all of the goods in some cases. Overall, the directory delivers an overview of the industry as never before.

IS IT RIGHT FOR MY SITE?

Choosing the right program can be a laborious process. Focus on quality merchants that offer attractive commissions. Look for programs and products that:

• Are closely aligned with the subject matter of your Web site.

- Offer terms that have the potential to produce a respectable return.
- Pay for performance—as your site's sales level increases, so too should the commission fees.
- Provide a variety of linking methods, the most attractive being direct product links.
- Deliver an advanced level of affiliate support. The best programs provide newsletters, program tips, even personal assistance.
- Allow you to purchase goods and services through your own links.
- Provide adequate reporting, preferably online.
- Feature low balance payout amounts and frequent pay schedules.

WHAT'S NOT ACCEPTABLE?

For your Web site to be accepted into most affiliate programs, the site must conform to certain criteria. While each program may use different wording, the intent is generally the same. Affiliate Web sites must not promote hate, bias, discrimination, violence, illegal activities, or pornography, and must not violate intellectual property rights or trademarks. Affiliate sites must meet generally accepted community standards. In other words, it has to play on Main Street.

A LAST WORD

This field is moving so fast, I feel as if I've painted a portrait of a speeding train. The companies and programs portrayed in these pages are subject to change, as companies are acquired and program details are adjusted. You should always read the fine print on each program before you put your electronic pen on the line.

Site Name	**1-800-FLOWERS.COM**
URL	http://www.1800flowers.com
Type of Goods or Services	Floral, gift, garden, home & gourmet goods
Email:	affiliate@1800flowers.com
Phone	516/237-6000
Snail Mail	1600 Stewart Ave., Westbury, NY 11590
Program Established	1997
Number of Affiliate Sites?	3,400—June 1999
Program Administration	LinkShare
Publically Traded?	Yes **Ticker:** FLWS
Revenues 1998	$300 Million+
Competitors	PC Flowers & Gifts, Proflowers, FTD
Commission Schedule	6% under $1,000 (monthly)
	6.5% $1,000–$1,999 (monthly)
	7% $2,000–$12,499 (monthly)
	8% over $12,500 (monthly)
Return Days	10
Payment Schedule	Quarterly
Payment If Over	$25
Type of Reporting	Online via LinkShare
Restrictions	
OK to Buy Through Link?	Yes
OK to Link to Competitors?	Yes
Highest Monthly Commission Paid to Date	N/A
High Sales Incentives?	Opportunity to lock in a higher permanent revenue share.
Additional Perks	Special offers from partners, advance notification of promotions, random acts of kindness, mention at PR-able events.

Site Name	1bookstreet.com
URL	http://www.1bookstreet.com
Type of Goods or Services	Bargain, out-of-print and remainder books. Specialty sites for mystery, romance, cooking and audio books.
Email:	jcon@1bookstreet.com
Phone	707/463-1351
Snail Mail	P.O. Box 8515, Ukiah, CA 95482
Program Established	September 1998
Number of Affiliate Sites?	5,000—June 1999
Program Administration	LinkShare/In-house administrator
Publically Traded?	No **Ticker:** N/A
Revenues 1998	$5 million
Competitors	bn.com, Amazon.com, Borders, Bookexpress.com
Commission Schedule	Tiered 20%, 10%, 5%
Full details at:	http://www.1bookstreet.com/Affiliate.asp
Return Days	60 days
Payment Schedule	Monthly
Payment If Over	$25
Type of Reporting	Online via LinkShare
Restrictions	Sites approved at the merchant's discretion.
OK to Buy Through Link?	Yes
OK to Link to Competitors?	Yes
Highest Monthly Commission Paid to Date	$600
High Sales Incentives?	Yes
Additional Perks	

Site Name	800.com
URL	http://www.800.com
Type of Goods or Services	Consumer electronics, movies, music.
Email:	Partners@800.com
Phone	800/327-5815 503/994-3600
Snail Mail	1516 NW Thurman, Portland, OR 97209
Program Established	July 1999
Number of Affiliate Sites?	N/A
Program Administration	Be Free/In-house
Publically Traded?	No **Ticker:** N/A
Revenues 1998	N/A
Competitors	Value America, Amazon.com, Electronics.net
Commission Schedule	8% - movies and music 4% - consumer electronics and accessories
Return Days	N/A
Payment Schedule	Quarterly
Payment If Over	$75
Type of Reporting	Online via Be Free
Restrictions	
OK to Buy Through Link?	Yes
OK to Link to Competitors?	Yes
Highest Monthly Commission Paid to Date	N/A
High Sales Incentives?	Yes
Additional Perks	Yes, for high sales customers.

Site Name	Amazon.com
URL	http://www.amazon.com
Type of Goods or Services	Books, music, video, gifts, toys, and auctions.
Email:	associates@amazon.com
Phone	206/622-2335
Snail Mail	1516 Second Ave., Seattle, WA 98101
Program Established	July 1996
Number of Affiliate Sites?	260,000—April 1999
Program Administration	In-house
Publically Traded?	Yes **Ticker:** AMZN
Revenues 1998	Net Sales over $600,000,000
Competitors	bn.com, Borders, Fatbrain, 1BookStreet, CDNOW, eToys, and others
Commission Schedule	15% for direct hit to individually linked books (sold at 10–30% of list) 5% for other qualifying books 5% for CDs, DVDs, toys, and videos 5% for consumer electronics (maximum of $10 per item)
Return Days	N/A
Payment Schedule	Quarterly
Payment If Over	$100
Type of Reporting	Email—weekly and quarterly
Restrictions	
OK to Buy Through Link?	No
OK to Link to Competitors?	Yes
Highest Monthly	
Commission Paid to Date	N/A
High Sales Incentives?	N/A
Additional Perks	T-shirts

Site Name	AmericanSpice.com
URL	http://www.americanspice.com
Type of Goods or Services	Over 3200 spices, spice blends and hot sauces
Email:	associates@americanspice.com
Phone	219/459-2521
Snail Mail	PO Box 8368, Fort Wayne, IN 46898-8368
Program Established	July 1998
Number of Affiliate Sites?	1,645—July 1999
Program Administration	In-house
Publically Traded?	No **Ticker:** N/A
Revenues 1998	N/A
Competitors	
Commission Schedule	10% from the original click-through which is paid for all purchases they make for a period of 12 months.
Return Days	60
Payment Schedule	Monthly
Payment If Over	$0
Type of Reporting	Email (online scheduled for Q4, 1999).
Restrictions	
OK to Buy Through Link?	Yes
OK to Link to Competitors?	Yes
Highest Monthly Commission Paid to Date	N/A
High Sales Incentives?	N/A
Additional Perks	N/A

Site Name	Art.com
URL	http://www.art.com
Type of Goods or Services	art
Email:	lstatland@art.com
Phone	847/362-2500
Snail Mail	13820 Polo Trail Drive, Lake Forest, IL 60045
Program Established	1997
Number of Affiliate Sites?	9,000—June 1999
Program Administration	LinkShare
Publically Traded?	Yes (subsidiary of Getty Images) **Ticker:** GETY
Revenues 1998	N/A
Competitors	barewalls.com
Commission Schedule	15% on sales 2% on sales from referred sites (during first 90 days).
Return Days	N/A
Payment Schedule	Monthly
Payment If Over	$50
Type of Reporting	Online via LinkShare
Restrictions	
OK to Buy Through Link?	Yes
OK to Link to Competitors?	N/A
Highest Monthly	
Commission Paid to Date	N/A
High Sales Incentives?	N/A
Additional Perks	Commissions can be converted to store credits at a rate of 1 to 1.25.

Site Name	ArtToday
URL	http://www.arttoday.com
Type of Goods or Services	clipart, fonts, photos, web images
Email:	peterg@zedcor.com
Phone	520/881-8101
Snail Mail	3420 N. Dodge Boulevard, Suite Z Tucson, AZ 85716-1469
Program Established	1996
Number of Affiliate Sites?	2,000—June 1999
Program Administration	In-house
Publically Traded?	Yes **Ticker:** IMSI
Revenues 1998	$60 million
Competitors	
Commission Schedule	10%+ (depending on volume)
Return Days	N/A
Payment Schedule	Monthly/Quarterly
Payment If Over	$50 monthly, quarterly, otherwise
Type of Reporting	Online
Restrictions	
OK to Buy Through Link?	Yes
OK to Link to Competitors?	Yes
Highest Monthly	
Commission Paid to Date	$5,000
High Sales Incentives?	Sliding commission scales, bonus incentives, etc. (Will negotiate with high-volume sites)
Additional Perks	N/A

Site Name	Astrology.net's ChartShop
URL	http://www.chartshop.com
Type of Goods or Services	Astrological reports
Email:	kimg@astrology.net
Phone	415/447-6193 x885
Snail Mail	PO Box 591692, San Francisco, CA 94159
Program Established	August 1996
Number of Affiliate Sites?	Direct affiliates: 300 (total sites 5,000+)—June 1999
Program Administration	Commission Junction/In-house (moving to 100% CJ)
Publically Traded?	Yes (Part of iVillage) **Ticker:** IVIL
Revenues 1998	$15,000,000 (company-wide)
Competitors	AstroNet
Commission Schedule	12-20% of gross transaction value depending on volume
Return Days	180 days from initial and subsequent referral.
Payment Schedule	Monthly
Payment If Over	$25.00
Type of Reporting	CJ affiliates—Online. Direct affiliates—monthly email.
Restrictions	
OK to Buy Through Link?	Yes
OK to Link to Competitors?	Yes
Highest Monthly Commission Paid to Date	over $5,000
High Sales Incentives?	Affiliate commission percentage rises with sales volume.
Additional Perks	Sites with over 200,000 monthly pageviews (and some smaller focused sites) may license a broad range of content including daily horoscopes.

Site Name	Audio Book Club
URL	http://www.audiobookclub.com
Type of Goods or Services	recorded books
Email:	customerservice@audiobookclub.com
Phone	973/539-9528
Snail Mail	20 Community Place, Morristown, NJ 07962
Program Established	August 1998
Number of Affiliate Sites?	N/A
Program Administration	LinkShare/In-house
Publically Traded?	Yes **Ticker:** KLB
Revenues 1998	$22,242,155
Competitors	
Commission Schedule	$5 per new member
Return Days	5
Payment Schedule	Quarterly
Payment If Over	$5
Type of Reporting	Online via LinkShare
Restrictions	
OK to Buy Through Link?	Yes
OK to Link to Competitors?	No
Highest Monthly Commission Paid to Date	N/A
High Sales Incentives?	N/A
Additional Perks	N/A

Site Name	AutoAccessory.com
URL	http://www.autoaccessory.com
Type of Goods or Services	Auto accessories for cars, trucks and SUV's.
Email:	info@ecomworks.com
Phone	1-888/734-8734 or 949/221-8600
Snail Mail	17975 Sky Park Circle, Irvine, CA 92614
Program Established	April 1999
Number of Affiliate Sites?	N/A
Program Administration	LinkShare/EcomWorks
Publically Traded?	No **Ticker:** N/A
Revenues 1998	N/A
Competitors	
Commission Schedule	10%
Return Days	45
Payment Schedule	Quarterly
Payment If Over	$100
Type of Reporting	Online via LinkShare
Restrictions	
OK to Buy Through Link?	Yes
OK to Link to Competitors?	No
Highest Monthly	
Commission Paid to Date	N/A
High Sales Incentives?	N/A
Additional Perks	N/A

Site Name	autoweb.com
URL	http://www.autoweb.com
Type of Goods or Services	everything for autos on the web
Email:	colbyg@autoweb.com
Phone	408/330-4744
Snail Mail	3270 Jay St., Santa Clara, CA 95054
Program Established	October 1995
Number of Affiliate Sites?	4,200—May 1999
Program Administration	In-house
Publically Traded?	Yes **Ticker:** AWEB
Revenues 1998	$13 million
Competitors	Carpoint, Autobytel, CarPrices
Commission Schedule	$2.00 for purchase requests $5.00 for private owner listings(less any credits issued)
Return Days	N/A
Payment Schedule	Monthly
Payment If Over	$50
Type of Reporting	
Restrictions	Any sites with objectionable materials
OK to Buy Through Link?	Yes
OK to Link to Competitors?	Yes
Highest Monthly Commission Paid to Date	$10,000+
High Sales Incentives?	N/A
Additional Perks	Cobranded content.

Site Name	Avon
URL	http://www.avon.com
Type of Goods or Services	beauty
Email:	dearavon@avon.com
Phone	N/A
Snail Mail	1251 Ave. of the Americas, New York, NY 10020
Program Established	1998
Number of Affiliate Sites?	N/A
Program Administration	LinkShare
Publically Traded?	Yes **Ticker:** AVP
Revenues 1998	$5 Billion
Competitors	
Commission Schedule	8%
Return Days	0
Payment Schedule	6x per year
Payment If Over	?
Type of Reporting	Online via LinkShare
Restrictions	Affiliates must be based in the U.S.
OK to Buy Through Link?	N/A
OK to Link to Competitors?	N/A
Highest Monthly	
Commission Paid to Date	N/A
High Sales Incentives?	N/A
Additional Perks	N/A

Site Name	BabyCenter.com
URL	http://www.babycenter.com
Type of Goods or Services	baby and maternity products
Email:	store@babycenter.com
Phone	877/551-2229
Snail Mail	539 Bryant St., Suite 200, San Francisco, CA 94107
Program Established	December 1998
Number of Affiliate Sites?	3,500—May 1999
Program Administration	Be Free/In-house
Publically Traded?	Yes (acquired by eToys) **Ticker:** ETYS
Revenues 1998	N/A
Competitors	baby, babiesrus.com, babysupermall.com
Commission Schedule	15% (20% if signed up during January 1999)
Return Days	N/A
Payment Schedule	Quarterly
Payment If Over	$50
Type of Reporting	Online via BeFree
Restrictions	
OK to Buy Through Link?	Yes
OK to Link to Competitors?	Yes
Highest Monthly Commission Paid to Date	$1,000
High Sales Incentives?	N/A
Additional Perks	"Buying through your own link is a pretty big perk especially since it's 15% off!"

Site Name	Barewalls.com
URL	http://www.barewalls.com
Type of Goods or Services	Art prints, posters and lithographs
Email:	info@barewalls.com
Phone	800/455-3955
Snail Mail	55 Massachusetts Ave., Cambridge, MA 02139-3180
Program Established	September 1998
Number of Affiliate Sites?	1,000+ —June 1999
Program Administration	In-house
Publically Traded?	No **Ticker:** N/A
Revenues 1998	N/A
Competitors	Printfinity, Art, ArtSelect
Commission Schedule	18% for direct-to-product referrals 15% for all other referrals 2% of recommended affiliate site sales (90 days)
Return Days	30
Payment Schedule	Monthly
Payment If Over	$50
Type of Reporting	Email (weekly)
Restrictions	
OK to Buy Through Link?	Yes
OK to Link to Competitors?	Yes
Highest Monthly	
Commission Paid to Date	$150
High Sales Incentives?	N/A
Additional Perks	Bonus store credit, additional discounts if commissions are used to buy merchandise.

Site Name	barnesandnoble.com
URL	http://www.bn.com
Type of Goods or Services	Books, music, and related information products
Email:	affiliatehelp@barnesandnoble.com
Phone	212/414-6000
Snail Mail	76 Ninth Ave., 11th floor, New York, NY 10011
Program Established	September 1997
Number of Affiliate Sites?	160,000—July 1999
Program Administration	BeFree/in-house
Publically Traded?	Yes **Ticker:** BNBN
Revenues 1998	$61.8 million
Competitors	amazon.com, borders.com, cdnow.com, etc.
Commission Schedule	Books, magazines, and videos— 5% below $20,000, 6% above $20,000 7% above $1,000,000 Gift certificates, music, and software: 5%
Return Days	N/A
Payment Schedule	Quarterly
Payment If Over	$100
Type of Reporting	Online via Be Free
Restrictions	
OK to Buy Through Link?	Yes
OK to Link to Competitors?	No
Highest Monthly	
Commission Paid to Date	N/A
High Sales Incentives?	Yes
Additional Perks	N/A

Site Name	Beyond.com
URL	http://www.beyond.com
Type of Goods or Services	Software, hardware, and peripherals
Email:	affiliates@beyond.com
Phone	408/616-4200
Snail Mail	1195 West Fremont Ave., Sunnyvale, CA 94087
Program Established	May 1998
Number of Affiliate Sites?	45,000—September 1999
Program Administration	In-house
Publically Traded?	Yes **Ticker:** BYND
Revenues 1998	$36.7 million
Competitors	
Commission Schedule	2% hardware 5% packaged software 10% downloadable software
Return Days	30
Payment Schedule	Quarterly
Payment If Over	$75
Type of Reporting	Online real-time, semi-monthly email
Restrictions	
OK to Buy Through Link?	Yes
OK to Link to Competitors?	Depending on level
Highest Monthly	
Commission Paid to Date	N/A
High Sales Incentives?	Yes
Additional Perks	Sales incentive program, exclusive offers, and URL identifiers to track purchases from multiple links.

Site Name	Borders
URL	http://www.borders.com
Type of Goods or Services	Books, music, videos
Email:	associates@borders.com
Phone	734/477-1180
Snail Mail	Borders Online, Inc., 100 Phoenix Drive, Ann Arbor, MI 48108
Program Established	March 1999
Number of Affiliate Sites?	5,000—June 1999
Program Administration	LinkShare
Publically Traded?	Yes **Ticker:** BGP
Revenues 1998	$4 million (online)
Competitors	bn.com, Amazon.com, CDNOW
Commission Schedule	5% from $0 to $20,000 6% from $20,000.01 to $1,000,000 7% from $1,000,000.01 onwards
Return Days	N/A
Payment Schedule	Quarterly
Payment If Over	$50
Type of Reporting	Online via LinkShare
Restrictions	
OK to Buy Through Link?	Yes
OK to Link to Competitors?	Yes
Highest Monthly Commission Paid to Date	N/A
High Sales Incentives?	Commission scale
Additional Perks	N/A

Site Name	Bottomdollar.com
URL	http://www.bottomdollar. com
Type of Goods or Services	Retail products price comparison
Email:	info@bottomdollar.com
Phone	316/636-9150
Snail Mail	8200 E. 34th St. Circle N. Bldg 1000, Suite 1001, Wichita, KS 67226
Program Established	July 1997
Number of Affiliate Sites?	1,000+ —June 1999
Program Administration	In-house
Publically Traded?	No **Ticker:** N/A
Revenues 1998	N/A
Competitors	mySimon
Commission Schedule	$0.020- $0.125 per click-through $5 per 1,000 page views on search results Complete revenue sharing plan can be found at http://www.bottomdollar.com/bdn/bdnrevenue.html
Return Days	N/A
Payment Schedule	Quarterly
Payment If Over	$20
Type of Reporting	Weekly email
Restrictions	No minors. Must pass shopping contents criteria.
OK to Buy Through Link?	Yes
OK to Link to Competitors?	Yes
Highest Monthly Commission Paid to Date	N/A
High Sales Incentives?	Cobranding or private labeling if traffic requirements are met.
Additional Perks	N/A

Site Name	CarClub.com
URL	http://www.carclub.com
Type of Goods or Services	Auto info, products and services, including: new and used car referral, vehicle inspection, factory order, personal shopper, multiple quotes, loan and lease applications
Email:	affiliates@carclub.com
Phone	1-800-CarClub
Snail Mail	221 Main St., Suite 250, San Francisco, CA 94105
Program Established	May 1999
Number of Affiliate Sites?	2,100—June 1999
Program Administration	Be Free
Publically Traded?	No **Ticker:** N/A
Revenues 1998	N/A
Competitors	1StopAuto, AutoWeb, Stoneage, AutoFusion, Priceline
Commission Schedule	Car quotes: new $2.00/used $0.50 Quick quotes $7.50 Personal shopper $12.50 Factory order $12.50 Lease $25.00, Inspection $5.00 Insurance quotes $0.15 per click
Return Days	N/A
Payment Schedule	Quarterly
Payment If Over	$75
Type of Reporting	Online via Be Free
Restrictions	
OK to Buy Through Link?	Yes
OK to Link to Competitors?	No
Highest Monthly Commission Paid to Date	N/A
High Sales Incentives?	Not yet available
Additional Perks	Not yet available

Site Name	CarPrices.com
URL	http://www.carprices.com
Type of Goods or Services	Free new car price quotes, free insurance quotes, free finance quotes, new and used car prices, auto related tips, new car information—reviews—rebates, free brochures, used car information, classifieds, and more.
Email:	nikki@autofusion.com
Phone	619/270-9444
Snail Mail	1940 Garnet Ave., Suite 104 Pacific Beach, CA 92109
Program Established	May 1998
Number of Affiliate Sites?	12,020 total—June 1999
Program Administration	In-house—9160, ClickTrade—613, BeFree-2247 affiliates.
Publically Traded?	No **Ticker:** N/A
Revenues 1998	Confidential
Competitors	Autoweb
Commission Schedule	New car price quotes—$3.00 Insurance quotes request—$1.20 Finance quote request—$2.50
Return Days	N/A
Payment Schedule	Quarterly
Payment If Over	$10
Type of Reporting	Online—real time
Restrictions	Agents cannot sign up as their own affiliate.
OK to Buy Through Link?	Yes
OK to Link to Competitors?	No
Highest Monthly Commission Paid to Date	$2,200
High Sales Incentives?	High traffic sites are given the opprotunity to become Private Label sites.
Additional Perks	Agent program allows webmasters to earn 10% of all referred affiliates' commissions.

Site Name	CBS SportsLine
URL	http://www.sportsline.com
Type of Goods or Services	Sporting goods, golf products, and sports collectibles.
Email:	pinzon@sportsline.com
Phone	954/351-2120 x7813
Snail Mail	6340 NW 5th Way, Fort Lauderdale, FL 33309
Program Established	January 1999
Number of Affiliate Sites?	3,500—May 1999
Program Administration	LinkShare
Publically Traded?	Yes **Ticker:** SPLN
Revenues 1998	$50 million
Competitors	ESPN
Commission Schedule	5% and up
Return Days	varies—24 hours and up
Payment Schedule	Monthly
Payment If Over	$25
Type of Reporting	Online via LinkShare
Restrictions	
OK to Buy Through Link?	Yes
OK to Link to Competitors?	Yes, although exclusive affiliates are entitled to benefits
Highest Monthly	
Commission Paid to Date	Approx. $150
High Sales Incentives?	Yes
Additional Perks	Website reviews and personalized selling tips and incentives.

Site Name	CDNOW
URL	http://cdnow.com/cosmic
Type of Goods or Services	Music retail
Email:	cosmicmail@cdnow.com
Phone	215/619-9900
Snail Mail	1005 Virginia Drive, Fort Washington, PA 19034
Program Established	March 1997
Number of Affiliate Sites?	210,000+ —May 1999
Program Administration	In-house
Publically Traded?	Yes **Ticker:** CDNW
Revenues 1998	56.4 million
Competitors	Amazon.com

Commission Schedule	Monthly Revenues	Comm. for That Month
	0–$499.99	7%
	$500.00–$1,499.99	8%
	$1,500.00–$2,999.99	9%
	$3,000.00–$4,999.99	10%
	$5,000.00–$7,999.99	11%
	$8,000.00–$10,999.99	12%
	$11,000.00–$13,999.99	13%
	$14,000.00–$16,999.99	14%
	$17,000.00 and over	15%*
	*Bonus commission	

Return Days	N/A
Payment Schedule	Quarterly
Payment If Over	$100
Type of Reporting	online and email (updated weekly)
Restriction	Commission paid in US Dollars only
OK to Buy Through Link?	Yes
OK to Link to Competitors?	Yes
Highest Monthly Commission Paid to Date	N/A
High Sales Incentives?	Higher commissions
Additional Perks	frequent discounts to post on site (to offer to visitors and promote sales), store and band contests/promotions run at all times in the members section

Site Name	chipshot.com
URL	http://www.chipshot.com
Type of Goods or Services	Brand name and custom built golf clubs and accessories.
Email:	echavez@chipshot.com
Phone	408/746-0700
Snail Mail	1452 Kifer Road, Sunnyvale, CA 94086
Program Established	January 1998
Number of Affiliate Sites?	5,000+—June 1999
Program Administration	Be Free (was inhouse)
Publically Traded?	No **Ticker:** N/A
Revenues 1998	NA
Competitors	
Commission Schedule	20% - accessories 20% - chipshot.com custom built clubs 20% - components 1% - name brand products
Return Days	N/A
Payment Schedule	Quarterly
Payment If Over	$0
Type of Reporting	Online via Be Free
Restrictions	
OK to Buy Through Link?	Yes
OK to Link to Competitors?	"OK, but we don't like it!"
Highest Monthly Commission Paid to Date	$370
High Sales Incentives?	Yes
Additional Perks	Partner Rewards program is an incentive program rewarding the best performing affiliate sites per month and quarter.

Site Name	Cooking.com
URL	http://www.cooking.com
Type of Goods or Services	Bakeware, cookware, cutlery, gift baskets, housewares, specialty foods, etc.
Email:	info@ecomworks.com
Phone	914/479-0250
Snail Mail	2850 Ocean Park Blvd., Suite 310, Santa Monica, CA 90405
Program Established	June 1999
Number of Affiliate Sites?	N/A
Program Administration	LinkShare/EcomWorks
Publically Traded?	No **Ticker:** N/A
Revenues 1998	N/A
Competitors	Tavolo.com
Commission Schedule	20% until Dec. 31, 1999, then 10%
Return Days	30
Payment Schedule	Quarterly
Payment If Over	$100
Type of Reporting	Online via LinkShare
Restrictions	
OK to Buy Through Link?	Yes
OK to Link to Competitors?	No
Highest Monthly	
Commission Paid to Date	N/A
High Sales Incentives?	N/A
Additional Perks	N/A

Site Name	Creditland.com
URL	http://www.creditland.com
Type of Goods or Services	Home loans, credit cards, auto loans, personal loans
Email:	sean@creditland.com
Phone	415/551-2104
Snail Mail	1475 Folsom, Suite 300, San Francisco, CA 94103
Program Established	April 1999
Number of Affiliate Sites?	800—June 1999
Program Administration	LinkShare/In-house (2 person team)
Publically Traded?	No **Ticker:** N/A
Revenues 1998	N/A
Competitors	NextCard, LendingTree, E-loan
Commission Schedule	Approved applications Credit Cards: $10 Home Loans: $25 Auto Loans: $15
Return Days	N/A
Payment Schedule	Quarterly
Payment If Over	$25
Type of Reporting	Online via LinkShare
Restrictions	
OK to Buy Through Link?	N/A
OK to Link to Competitors?	No
Highest Monthly	
Commission Paid to Date	N/A
High Sales Incentives?	N/A
Additional Perks	N/A

Site Name	Delia's
URL	http://www.delias.com
Type of Goods or Services	Girls and young women's clothing, accessories, cosmetics, roomwares, etc.
Email:	affiliatesupport@delias.com
Phone	1-800-DELIANY
Snail Mail	N/A
Program Established	April 1999
Number of Affiliate Sites?	Over 7,000—July 1999
Program Administration	LinkShare/In-house
Publically Traded?	Yes **Ticker:** TURF
Revenues 1998	N/A
Competitors	JCrew.com, Gap.com, others
Commission Schedule	5%
Return Days	0
Payment Schedule	Quarterly
Payment If Over	$25
Type of Reporting	Online via LinkShare/Private network for partners
Restriction	Domestic orders only.
OK to Buy Through Link?	Yes
OK to Link to Competitors?	Yes
Highest Monthly Commission Paid to Date	N/A
High Sales Incentives?	In the works.
Additional Perks	In the works.

Site Name eBags

URL	http://www.ebags.com
Type of Goods or Services	Bags and accessories for business sports and travel.
Email:	ambassadors@ebags.com
Phone	303/694-1933
Snail Mail	6060 Greenwood Plaza Boulevard, Greenwood Village, CO 80111
Program Established	April 1999
Number of Affiliate Sites?	3,000—June 1999
Program Administration	Be Free/In-house
Publically Traded?	No **Ticker:** N/A
Revenues 1998	N/A
Competitors	
Commission Schedule	Up to $25,000—7% $25,000 to $100,000—8% Over $100,000—10%
Return Days	N/A
Payment Schedule	Quarterly
Payment If Over	$25
Type of Reporting	Online via Be Free
Restrictions	Site must contain original content.
OK to Buy Through Link?	Yes
OK to Link to Competitors?	Yes
Highest Monthly Commission Paid to Date	N/A
High Sales Incentives?	Sliding commission scale.
Additional Perks	In the works.

Site Name	electronics.net
URL	http://electronics.net
Type of Goods or Services	Consumer electronics and appliances (Joint-venture parent companies—Cybershop.com and Tops Appliance City)
Email:	feedback@electronics.net
Phone	888/760-6321
Snail Mail	116 Newark Ave., Jersey City, NJ 07302
Program Established	December 1998
Number of Affiliate Sites?	5,000—June 1999
Program Administration	LinkShare/In-house
Publically Traded?	Yes—CYSP and TOPS **Ticker:**
Revenues 1998	Cybershop.com—$4.8 million
Competitors	BestBuys, Circuit City, 800.com, GoodGuys, NetMarket, Crutchfield
Commission Schedule	4%
Return Days	10
Payment Schedule	Quarterly
Payment If Over	No minimum
Type of Reporting	Online via LinkShare
Restrictions	
OK to Buy Through Link?	Yes
OK to Link to Competitors?	Yes
Highest Monthly Commission Paid to Date	N/A
High Sales Incentives?	N/A
Additional Perks	N/A

Site Name	Enews.com (formerly Electronic Newsstand)
URL	http://www.enews.com
Type of Goods or Services	magazine subscriptions
Email:	tspalmer@enews.com
Phone	202/466-8688
Snail Mail	1225 19th St. NW, Suite 400, Washington, DC 20036
Program Established	August 1997
Number of Affiliate Sites?	16,000—May 1999
Program Administration	Be Free/In-house
Publically Traded?	No **Ticker:** N/A
Revenues 1998	N/A
Competitors	Publishers Clearing House, Magmall
Commission Schedule	10%, 15%, 20% (volume dependant)
Return Days	N/A
Payment Schedule	Quarterly
Payment If Over	$100
Type of Reporting	Online via Be Free
Restrictions	
OK to Buy Through Link?	Yes
OK to Link to Competitors?	Yes
Highest Monthly Commission Paid to Date	$2,000
High Sales Incentives?	Cash bonus and higher commission rate.
Additional Perks	N/A

Site Name	EPage Free Auctions & Classifieds
URL	http://ep.com/
Type of Goods or Services	Online classified and auctions
Email:	epage@ep.com
Phone	310/316-7424
Snail Mail	1815 Via el Prado, Suite 203 Redondo Beach, CA 90277
Program Established	April 1996, CSP—August 1997, Referral—May 1998
Number of Affiliate Sites?	CSP: 10,793, Referral: 1,821
Program Administration	100% in-house
Publically Traded?	No **Ticker:** N/A
Revenues 1998	N/A
Competitors	UBid, eBay, Classifieds2000, AdOne, Amazon Auctions, Yahoo Classifieds
Commission Schedule	CSP: 20% of gross on all ads posted through their site Referral: 10% of gross on all ads posted from users referred by the Affiliate, for life Note: Affiliates can join both for a 30% initial, and 10% lifetime residual
Return Days	N/A
Payment Schedule	Monthly
Payment If Over	$20
Type of Reporting	Online real-time and weekly email
Restrictions	
OK to Buy Through Link?	Yes
OK to Link to Competitors?	Yes
Highest Monthly Commission Paid to Date	$314.43
High Sales Incentives?	No
Additional Perks	None

Site Name	ESPRIT
URL	http://www.exprit.com
Type of Goods or Services	Girls' and women's clothing
Email:	affiliates@esprit.com
Phone	415/648-6900
Snail Mail	900 Minnesota, San Francisco, CA 94107
Program Established	1999
Number of Affiliate Sites?	N/A
Program Administration	LinkShare
Publically Traded?	N/A **Ticker:** N/A
Revenues 1998	N/A
Competitors	
Commission Schedule	7%
Return Days	0
Payment Schedule	Quarterly
Payment If Over	$100
Type of Reporting	Online via LinkShare
Restrictions	
OK to Buy Through Link?	N/A
OK to Link to Competitors?	N/A
Highest Monthly Commission Paid to Date	N/A
High Sales Incentives?	N/A
Additional Perks	

Site Name	eToys
URL	http://www.etoys.com
Type of Goods or Services	Toys, software, video games, music, videos, and baby products.
Email:	affiliates@etoys.com
Phone	310/664-8100
Snail Mail	3100 Ocean Park Boulevard, Suite 300, Santa Monica, CA
Program Established	January 1998
Number of Affiliate Sites?	10,000—June 1999
Program Administration	Be Free
Publically Traded?	Yes **Ticker:** ETYS
Revenues 1998	$30 million
Competitors	Amazon.com, KBKids.com, SmarterKids.com
Commission Schedule	5%-12.5% plus $5 bounty per each new customer
Return Days	N/A
Payment Schedule	Quarterly
Payment If Over	$20
Type of Reporting	Online via Be Free
Restrictions	Web site content must be "child-safe," U.S. sites only (at this moment).
OK to Buy Through Link?	Yes
OK to Link to Competitors?	Yes
Highest Monthly Commission Paid to Date	N/A
High Sales Incentives?	Higher commission (sliding scale)
Additional Perks	N/A

Site Name	**Fatbrain.com (formerly Computer Literacy)**
URL	http://www.fatbrain.com
Type of Goods or Services	computer books, interactive training, documentation
Email:	affiliates@fatbrain.com
Phone	408/541-2020
Snail Mail	2550 Walsh Ave., Santa Clara, CA 95051
Program Established	May 1997
Number of Affiliate Sites?	4,500—May 1998
Program Administration	currently in-house, will be 3rd party
Publically Traded?	Yes **Ticker:** FATB
Revenues 1998	$19.8 million
Competitors	Amazon.com, barnesandnoble.com, Borders.com, Rowe.com
Commission Schedule	20% for directly linked-to titles 10% for interactive training 5% for all other referred sales
Return Days	N/A
Payment Schedule	Quarterly
Payment If Over	$30
Type of Reporting	Online
Restrictions	
OK to Buy Through Link?	Yes
OK to Link to Competitors?	Yes
Highest Monthly Commission Paid to Date	$2,000
High Sales Incentives?	None (yet)
Additional Perks	Promotions to/through affiliates

Site Name	FirstPlace Software, Inc.
URL	http://www.webposition.com
Type of Goods or Services	WebPosition Gold—search engine marketing software
Email:	sales@webposition.com
Phone	800/962-4855
Snail Mail	PO Box 3774, Joplin, MO 64803
Program Established	August 1997
Number of Affiliate Sites?	9,700—June 1999 (9,000 partners/700 dealers)
Program Administration	In-house
Publically Traded?	No **Ticker:** N/A
Revenues 1998	$1.6 million
Competitors	No direct competition, presently. (Submission or rank reporting tools are the closest.)
Commission Schedule	15% for referral partners. 30-40% for dealers. See: http://www.webposition.com/partner.htm
Return Days	N/A
Payment Schedule	$40 or 3 months, whichever comes first.
Payment If Over	see above
Type of Reporting	Monthly online (email sent when stats are posted).
Restrictions	Dealer level requires software purchase (45-day money back guarantee).
OK to Buy Through Link?	Yes
OK to Link to Competitors?	Yes
Highest Monthly Commission Paid to Date	$2,500
High Sales Incentives?	Dealer program offers larger percentages with volume.
Additional Perks	FirstPlace refers people back to your site via email after they download the product.

Site Name	Fogdog Sports
URL	http://www.fogdog.com
Type of Goods or Services	Sporting goods, equipment, apparel, and footwear.
Email:	michael@fogdog.com
Phone	650/980-2500
Snail Mail	500 Broadway, Redwood City, CA 94063
Program Established	October 1998
Number of Affiliate Sites?	40,000—June 1999
Program Administration	Be Free
Publically Traded?	No **Ticker:** N/A
Revenues 1998	N/A
Competitors	REI, chipshot.com, Sports Superstore, Dick's
Commission Schedule	10%-20% depending on sales volume.
Return Days	24 hours
Payment Schedule	Quarterly
Payment If Over	$100 (currently re-evaluating)
Type of Reporting	Online via Be Free
Restrictions	
OK to Buy Through Link?	Yes
OK to Link to Competitors?	Yes
Highest Monthly Commission Paid to Date	"Can't say, but it's high."
High Sales Incentives?	20% commissions at highest level. Affiliate sales promotions have included a $5,000 adventure travel trip to Cost Rica and other prizes.
Additional Perks	Yes

Site Name	FragranceNet.com
URL	http://www.fragrancenet.com
Type of Goods or Services	Over 1,000 brand name fragrances, including: Bijan, Giorgio, Ralph Lauren, and Calvin Klein.
Email:	info@fragrancenet.com
Phone	800/987-3738 or 516/242-3205
Snail Mail	2070 Deer Park Ave., Deer Park, NY 11729
Program Established	1997
Number of Affiliate Sites?	Over 7,000—June 1999
Program Administration	LinkShare
Publically Traded?	No **Ticker:** N/A
Revenues 1998	N/A
Competitors	Fragrance Counter
Commission Schedule	8% base rate
Return Days	0
Payment Schedule	Monthly
Payment If Over	$10
Type of Reporting	Online via LinkShare
Restrictions	
OK to Buy Through Link?	Yes
OK to Link to Competitors?	Yes
Highest Monthly Commission Paid to Date	N/A
High Sales Incentives?	"None to date but we have a program on the horizon."
Additional Perks	Offers free shopping, free gift wrapping, and a free gift with every order.

Site Name	FreeShop
URL	http://www.freeshop.com
Type of Goods or Services	Free & trial offers
Email:	associates@freeshop.com
Phone	206/441-9100
Snail Mail	95 South Jackson St., Suite 300, Seattle, WA 98104
Program Established	November 1998
Number of Affiliate Sites?	12,000—May 1999
Program Administration	LinkShare and ClickTrade
Publically Traded?	No **Ticker:** N/A
Revenues 1998	N/A
Competitors	FreeForum, CoolSavings, ENews, ValuPage, MyPoints, CatalogCity, and CatalogLink
Commission Schedule	30%:$1 to $500 40%: $501 to $1,000 50%: $1,001 and up $0.05 per click-through
Return Days	30
Payment Schedule	Monthly/Quarterly
Payment If Over	Over$10—monthly. Less that $10—quarterly.
Type of Reporting	Online via LinkShare and ClickTrade
Restrictions	
OK to Buy Through Link?	Yes
OK to Link to Competitors?	Yes
Highest Monthly Commission Paid to Date	Several thousand dollars
High Sales Incentives?	Increased commission levels.
Additional Perks	Also pays per click.

Site Name	Fridgedoor.com
URL	http://www.fridgedoor.com
Type of Goods or Services	Refrigerator magnets, gifts, novelties, licensed characters, collectibles, auctions
Email:	chris@fridgedoor.com
Phone	617/770-7913
Snail Mail	21 Dixwell Ave., Quincy, MA 02169
Program Established	N/A
Number of Affiliate Sites?	250 (and growing)—May 1999
Program Administration	In-house
Publically Traded?	No **Ticker:** N/A
Revenues 1998	N/A
Competitors	
Commission Schedule	15% of all sales from customers originating at their site
Return Days	30 days
Payment Schedule	Quarterly
Payment If Over	$25
Type of Reporting	Daily online reports
Restrictions	Site must be reviewed before approval is granted.
OK to Buy Through Link?	Yes
OK to Link to Competitors?	Yes
Highest Monthly Commission Paid to Date	N/A
High Sales Incentives?	Donate product for use in promotions on Affiliate site.
Additional Perks	N/A

Site Name	furniture.com
URL	http://www.furniture.com
Type of Goods or Services	Home furniture and furnishings
Email:	affiliate@furniture.com
Phone	508/416-6396
Snail Mail	1881 Worcester Road, Ste 2, Framingham, MA 01701
Program Established	June 1999
Number of Affiliate Sites?	New program
Program Administration	Be Free
Publically Traded?	No **Ticker:** N/A
Revenues 1998	N/A
Competitors	
Commission Schedule	$4.75 referral fee (first 100 per month) 5% commission
Return Days	30 days from initial registration
Payment Schedule	30 days
Payment If Over	$50
Type of Reporting	Online via Be Free
Restrictions	
OK to Buy Through Link?	Yes
OK to Link to Competitors?	Yes
Highest Monthly Commission Paid to Date	N/A
High Sales Incentives?	N/A
Additional Perks	N/A

Site Name	Genius Babies!
URL	http://www.GeniusBabies.com
Type of Goods or Services	Developmental Baby Gifts: toys, books, Baby Mozart & Baby Einstein videos & classical music for infants and toddlers.
Email:	info@GeniusBabies.com
Phone	770/457-1003
Snail Mail	1900 Harts Mill Road, Atlanta, GA 30341
Program Established	March 1999
Number of Affiliate Sites?	100+ —June 1999
Program Administration	Yahoo
Publically Traded?	No **Ticker:** N/A
Revenues 1998	N/A
Competitors	
Commission Schedule	10% (including repeat customers)
Return Days	N/A
Payment Schedule	Monthly
Payment If Over	$0
Type of Reporting	Online via Yahoo
Restrictions	
OK to Buy Through Link?	Yes
OK to Link to Competitors?	Yes
Highest Monthly Commission Paid to Date	$200
High Sales Incentives?	To be added
Additional Perks	N/A

Site Name	Giftpoint.com
URL	http://www.giftpoint.com
Type of Goods or Services	Paper and e-gift certificates from over 220 retailers, restaurants, shops and Internet "e-tailers." Gift certificates can be sent via hard copy or electronically via e-mail. Also offers the "Giftpoint Certificate" which can be redeemed at participating retailers.
Email:	affiliate@giftpoint.com
Phone	402/445-2300
Snail Mail	11510 Blondo St., Suite 103, Omaha, NE 68164
Program Established	May 1999
Number of Affiliate Sites?	3,100—June 1999
Program Administration	Be Free
Publically Traded?	No **Ticker:** N/A
Revenues 1998	N/A
Competitors	
Commission Schedule	$3.00 per customer sale
Return Days	N/A
Payment Schedule	Quarterly
Payment If Over	$50
Type of Reporting	Online via Be Free
Restrictions	
OK to Buy Through Link?	Yes
OK to Link to Competitors?	Not recommended
Highest Monthly Commission Paid to Date	Not disclosed
High Sales Incentives?	Case by case
Additional Perks	Case by case

Site Name	healthshop.com
URL	http://www.healthshop.com
Type of Goods or Services	natural health store offering over 6,000 products at prices 20-40% below retail
Email:	affiliates@healthshop.com
Phone	415/908-1801
Snail Mail	568 Howard St., Lower Level, San Francisco, CA 94105
Program Established	May 1999
Number of Affiliate Sites?	1,000—June 1999
Program Administration	LinkShare
Publically Traded?	No **Ticker:** N/A
Revenues 1998	N/A
Competitors	More.com, MotherNature.com
Commission Schedule	15% commission, plus $0.01 per click-through
Return Days	0
Payment Schedule	Quarterly
Payment If Over	$50
Type of Reporting	Online via LinkShare
Restrictions	
OK to Buy Through Link?	Yes
OK to Link to Competitors?	Yes
Highest Monthly Commission Paid to Date	N/A
High Sales Incentives?	N/A
Additional Perks	N/A

Site Name	Hickory Farms
URL	http://www.hickoryfarms.com
Type of Goods or Services	Gourmet Foods and Gifts
Email:	agrid@hickoryfarms.com
Phone	419/893-7611
Snail Mail	1505 Holland Road, Maumee, OH 43537
Program Established	April 1999
Number of Affiliate Sites?	5,000+ —June 1999
Program Administration	LinkShare
Publically Traded?	No **Ticker:** N/A
Revenues 1998	N/A
Competitors	
Commission Schedule	7%
Return Days	30
Payment Schedule	Quarterly
Payment If Over	$25
Type of Reporting	Online via LinkShare
Restrictions	Hickory Farms must approve all affiliates.
OK to Buy Through Link?	Yes
OK to Link to Competitors?	Yes
Highest Monthly Commission Paid to Date	N/A
High Sales Incentives?	N/A
Additional Perks	N/A

Site Name	HostAmerica
URL	http://www.hostamerica.com/
Type of Goods or Services	web hosting
Email:	affiliate@hostamerica.com
Phone	877/HOST-999
Snail Mail	64 Perimeter Center East, Atlanta, GA 30346
Program Established	September 1998
Number of Affiliate Sites?	5,000 (approx.)—June 1999
Program Administration	LinkShare
Publically Traded?	No **Ticker:** N/A
Revenues 1998	N/A
Competitors	Verio, many others
Commission Schedule	1. $10 + 10% of monthly recurring revenue 2. $50 flat fee
Return Days	10
Payment Schedule	Monthly
Payment If Over	$50
Type of Reporting	Online via LinkShare
Restrictions	
OK to Buy Through Link?	Yes
OK to Link to Competitors?	N/A
Highest Monthly	
Commission Paid to Date	N/A
High Sales Incentives?	N/A
Additional Perks	N/A

Site Name	HotHotHot.com
URL	http://www.hothothot.com
Type of Goods or Services	Fiery foods, including hot sauces, BBQ sauces, and salsas.
Email:	hothothot@hothothot.com
Phone	800/959-7742
Snail Mail	
Program Established	End 1996
Number of Affiliate Sites?	2,000—June 1999
Program Administration	In-house
Publically Traded?	No **Ticker:** N/A
Revenues 1998	200K
Competitors	
Commission Schedule	5%-10%
Return Days	30 days
Payment Schedule	Monthly
Payment If Over	$50
Type of Reporting	Online (monthly)
Restrictions	
OK to Buy Through Link?	Yes
OK to Link to Competitors?	No
Highest Monthly Commission Paid to Date	$1,000
High Sales Incentives?	Quarterly Promotions—double commissions.
Additional Perks	Special Freebies to associates and an incentive every 3 months.

Site Name	i/us: all things graphic
URL	http://www.i-us.com
Type of Goods or Services	Web and print graphics and publishing software
Email:	affiliates@i-us.com
Phone	613/569-2949
Snail Mail	56 Sparks St., Suite 612, Ottawa, Ontario, Canada, K1P5A9
Program Established	January 1999
Number of Affiliate Sites?	8,245—June 1999
Program Administration	Be Free
Publically Traded?	No **Ticker:** N/A
Revenues 1998	N/A
Competitors	No direct competitors
Commission Schedule	10% on all software downloads (which constitutes 80% of the product offering) 5% on all physical products
Return Days	N/A
Payment Schedule	Quarterly
Payment If Over	$50
Type of Reporting	Online via Be Free
Restrictions	
OK to Buy Through Link?	Yes
OK to Link to Competitors?	Yes
Highest Monthly Commission Paid to Date	$455 US (for the quarter)—payments started in 4/99
High Sales Incentives?	N/A
Additional Perks	Has run sales contests where Affiliates could win an i/us polo shirt for the highest sales within a certain time period.

Site Name	iGoFish.com
URL	http://www.iGoFish.com
Type of Goods or Services	Fishing and fishing related merchandise
Email:	tomg@igofish.com
Phone	410/819-6800
Snail Mail	600 Dover Road, Suite 103, Easton MD 21601
Program Established	October 1998
Number of Affiliate Sites?	600—May 1999
Program Administration	In-house
Publically Traded?	No **Ticker:** N/A
Revenues 1998	N/A
Competitors	
Commission Schedule	Monthly sales 10% up to $150 12% $151-$400 15% $401+
Return Days	N/A
Payment Schedule	Quarterly
Payment If Over	$5
Type of Reporting	"Reel-time online"
Restrictions	N/A
OK to Buy Through Link?	Yes
OK to Link to Competitors?	Yes
Highest Monthly Commission Paid to Date	N/A
High Sales Incentives?	Currently 15%
Additional Perks	N/A

Site Name	Internet News Bureau
URL	http://www.newsbureau.com
Type of Goods or Services	Press release distribution service via email
Email:	info@newsbureau.com
Phone	888/699-6939
Snail Mail	600 SW Columbia, Suite 2100, Bend, OR 97702
Program Established	February 1998
Number of Affiliate Sites?	2,830—June 1999
Program Administration	In-house
Publically Traded?	No **Ticker:** N/A
Revenues 1998	N/A
Competitors	Business Wire, Url Wire, PR Newswire, Xpress Press
Commission Schedule	10%
Return Days	30
Payment Schedule	Monthly
Payment If Over	$20
Type of Reporting	Online
Restrictions	
OK to Buy Through Link?	Yes
OK to Link to Competitors?	Yes
Highest Monthly Commission Paid to Date	$200
High Sales Incentives?	No
Additional Perks	N/A

Site Name	iOwn.com
URL	http://www.iown.com
Type of Goods or Services	Online home mortgages and refinances as well as over 600,000 home listings for sale.
Email:	partners@iown.com
Phone	415/659-6896
Snail Mail	118 King St., Suite 260, San Francisco, CA 94107
Program Established	1996
Number of Affiliate Sites?	200+ —June 1999
Program Administration	In-house management and 3rd party software.
Publically Traded?	No **Ticker:** N/A
Revenues 1998	N/A
Competitors	ELoan, MS HomeAdvisor
Commission Schedule	Starts at $25.00 per submitted loan application
Return Days	N/A
Payment Schedule	Quarterly
Payment If Over	Negotiable
Type of Reporting	Reporting frequency varies based on needs of client
Restrictions	iOwn.com reserves the right to approve or disapprove any site for any reason.
OK to Buy Through Link?	Yes
OK to Link to Competitors?	Yes
Highest Monthly Commission Paid to Date	N/A
High Sales Incentives?	N/A
Additional Perks	N/A

Site Name	Jacques Morét
URL	http://www.moret.com
Type of Goods or Services	Women's and children's activewear
Email:	ashap@moret.com
Phone	212/354-2400
Snail Mail	1411 Broadway, New York, NY 10018
Program Established	May 1999
Number of Affiliate Sites?	1,258—June 1999
Program Administration	LinkShare/In-house
Publically Traded?	No **Ticker:** N/A
Revenues 1998	N/A
Competitors	Many smaller companies
Commission Schedule	12%
Return Days	5
Payment Schedule	Monthly
Payment If Over	$50
Type of Reporting	Online via LinkShare
Restrictions	
OK to Buy Through Link?	Not yet
OK to Link to Competitors?	No
Highest Monthly	
Commission Paid to Date	N/A
High Sales Incentives?	N/A
Additional Perks	N/A

Site Name	jcrew.com
URL	http://www.jcrew.com
Type of Goods or Services	men's and women's clothing
Email:	affiliate@jcrew.com
Phone	800/851/3189
Snail Mail	One Ivy Crescent, Lynchburg, VA 24513
Program Established	Summer 1998
Number of Affiliate Sites?	5,000—May 1999
Program Administration	In-house
Publically Traded?	No **Ticker:** N/A
Revenues 1998	N/A
Competitors	Gap, L.L. Bean, Land's End, Eddie Bauer
Commission Schedule	5% of sales—no credit for returns (20% of commission fee is held as reserve against product returns.)
Return Days	
Payment Schedule	Quarterly
Payment If Over	$250
Type of Reporting	Online
Restrictions	
OK to Buy Through Link?	Yes
OK to Link to Competitors?	Yes
Highest Monthly	
Commission Paid to Date	N/A
High Sales Incentives?	N/A
Additional Perks	N/A

Site Name	KBKids.com (formerly BrainPlay.com)
URL	http://www.KBKids.com
Type of Goods or Services	toys, video games, software, musical instruments, action figures
Email:	affiliates@KBKids.com
Phone	303/228-9000
Snail Mail	475 17th St, Suite 750, Denver, CO 80202
Program Established	January 1996
Number of Affiliate Sites?	1,500+ —May 1999
Program Administration	In-house
Publically Traded?	No **Ticker:** N/A
Revenues 1998	N/A
Competitors	Amazon.com, eToys.com, smarterkids.com
Commission Schedule	$10 per new customer
Return Days	N/A
Payment Schedule	Quarterly
Payment If Over	$100
Type of Reporting	Online, monthly
Restrictions	
OK to Buy Through Link?	Yes
OK to Link to Competitors?	Yes
Highest Monthly Commission Paid to Date	N/A
High Sales Incentives?	Yes
Additional Perks	Soon to be announced

Site Name	K-tel
URL	http://www.ktel.com
Type of Goods or Services	Music, custom music compilations (CDs)
Email:	affiliates@k-tel.com
Phone	800/266-7677
Snail Mail	23801 Calabasas Road #2000, Calabasas, CA 91302
Program Established	October 1998
Number of Affiliate Sites?	7,000—May 1999
Program Administration	LinkShare
Publically Traded?	Yes **Ticker:** KTEL
Revenues 1998	$85.6 million
Competitors	CDNOW, Amazon.com
Commission Schedule	10% Custom Compilations
10%   K-tel titles and subsidiary labels
All other music titles:
7%   0–$1,499
8% $1,500–$2,999
9% $3,000–$4,999
10%   over $4,999
Return Days	N/A
Payment Schedule	Quarterly
Payment If Over	$50
Type of Reporting	Online via LinkShare
Restrictions	
OK to Buy Through Link?	Yes
OK to Link to Competitors?	"Not really"
Highest Monthly Commission Paid to Date	N/A
High Sales Incentives?	N/A
Additional Perks	Commission structure is increased from time to time.

Site Name	LandscapeUSA
URL	http://www.landscapeusa.com
Type of Goods or Services	Landscaping, irrigation, and garden supplies
Email:	tim@landscapeusa.com
Phone	503/362-1033
Snail Mail	PO Box 5382/1510 Wallace Rd., NW, Salem, OR 97304
Program Established	November 1997
Number of Affiliate Sites?	4,500—June 1999
Program Administration	LinkShare
Publically Traded?	No **Ticker:** N/A
Revenues 1998	N/A
Competitors	garden.com, gardeners.com
Commission Schedule	8% standard 10% top-tier
Return Days	10 day standard, 30 day top-tier
Payment Schedule	Monthly
Payment If Over	$10
Type of Reporting	Online via LinkShare
Restrictions	Primarily ships to US and Canada. Publisher best served if audience is in North American market.
OK to Buy Through Link?	Yes
OK to Link to Competitors?	No
Highest Monthly Commission Paid to Date	N/A
High Sales Incentives?	Higher commission percentage
Additional Perks	"Nothing currently, but we have some things in the works."

Site Name	LendingTree
URL	http://www.lendingtree.com
Type of Goods or Services	Loan marketplace connecting consumers to a network of lenders who compete for their business. Products include: mortgages, home equity loans, personal loans, credit cards, auto loans
Email:	affiliates@lendingtree.com
Phone	704/541-5351
Snail Mail	6701 Carmel Road, Charlotte, NC 28226
Program Established	November 1998
Number of Affiliate Sites?	6,000—June 1999
Program Administration	Be Free/In-house
Publically Traded?	No **Ticker:** N/A
Revenues 1998	N/A
Competitors	ELoan, iOwn
Commission Schedule	Up to $14 per lead
Return Days	N/A
Payment Schedule	Monthly
Payment If Over	$30
Type of Reporting	Online via Be Free
Restrictions	
OK to Buy Through Link?	Yes
OK to Link to Competitors?	Yes, except for "Partners" sites
Highest Monthly Commission Paid to Date	$97,000
High Sales Incentives?	N/A
Additional Perks	Various goodies

Site Name	Liquor By Wire
URL	http://www.liquorbywire.com
Type of Goods or Services	Wine, champagne, spirits, and gift baskets
Email:	lbw@lbw.com
Phone	800/774-7483
Snail Mail	4205 West Irving Park Road, Chicago, IL 60641
Program Established	1997
Number of Affiliate Sites?	1,900 (approx.)—June 1999
Program Administration	LinkShare
Publically Traded?	No **Ticker:** N/A
Revenues 1998	N/A
Competitors	800 Spirits, SendWine.com, Wine.com
Commission Schedule	5–10%
Return Days	0
Payment Schedule	Monthly
Payment If Over	$100
Type of Reporting	Online via LinkShare
Restrictions	
OK to Buy Through Link?	Yes
OK to Link to Competitors?	No
Highest Monthly	
Commission Paid to Date	$3,000
High Sales Incentives?	N/A
Additional Perks	N/A

Site Name	More.com (formerly GreenTree Nutrition)
URL	http://www.greentree.com
Type of Goods or Services	vitamins, herbs
Email:	info@gtaffiliates.net
Phone	415/979-9597
Snail Mail	520 Third St., Suite 245, San Francisco, CA 94107
Program Established	N/A
Number of Affiliate Sites?	N/A
Program Administration	LinkShare/EcomWorks
Publically Traded?	N/A **Ticker:** N/A
Revenues 1998	N/A
Competitors	MotherNature.com, PlanetRX.com, DrugStore.com, SelfCare.com
Commission Schedule	15%
Return Days	0
Payment Schedule	Monthly
Payment If Over	$50
Type of Reporting	Online via LinkShare
Restrictions	
OK to Buy Through Link?	N/A
OK to Link to Competitors?	N/A
Highest Monthly	
Commission Paid to Date	N/A
High Sales Incentives?	N/A
Additional Perks	N/A

Site Name	MotherNature.com
URL	http://www.mothernature.com
Type of Goods or Services	Natural health products and information
Email:	affiliate@mothernature.com
Phone	978/929-2000
Snail Mail	One Concord Farms, 2nd Floor, 490 Virginia Road, Concord, MA 01742
Program Established	November 1998
Number of Affiliate Sites?	7,500+ —May 1999
Program Administration	Be Free
Publically Traded?	No **Ticker:** N/A
Revenues 1998	N/A
Competitors	More.com, VitaminShoppe.com, healthshop.com
Commission Schedule	20% per sale until December 31, 1999 12% per sale afterwards
Return Days	30 days
Payment Schedule	Quarterly
Payment If Over	$50
Type of Reporting	Online via Be Free
Restrictions	N/A
OK to Buy Through Link?	Yes
OK to Link to Competitors?	Yes
Highest Monthly Commission Paid to Date	N/A
High Sales Incentives?	N/A
Additional Perks	N/A

Site Name	mySimon
URL	http://www.mysimon.com
Type of Goods or Services	Comparison shopping featuring over 1,300 merchants in categories such as Computers, Books & Music, Electronics, Fashion, Flowers, Sporting Goods, Toys, and more. (13 different programs to pick from based on site's needs and interests.
Email:	webmaster@mysimon.com
Phone	408/330-4400
Snail Mail	2933 Bunker Hill Lane, Suite 202, Santa Clara, CA 95054
Program Established	May 1999
Number of Affiliate Sites?	200—June 1999
Program Administration	ClickTrade
Publically Traded?	No **Ticker:** N/A
Revenues 1998	N/A
Competitors	Junglee, Jango, Bottom Dollar
Commission Schedule	$0.08 per click to send users to homepage, $0.06 per click for other categories.
Return Days	N/A
Payment Schedule	Monthly
Payment If Over	$25
Type of Reporting	Online, real time
Restrictions	
OK to Buy Through Link?	Yes
OK to Link to Competitors?	Yes
Highest Monthly Commission Paid to Date	N/A
High Sales Incentives?	N/A
Additional Perks	N/A

Site Name	NaturalToys.com
URL	http://www.naturaltoys.com
Type of Goods or Services	Wood and natural fiber toys for children of all ages.
Email:	elves@naturaltoys.com
Phone	800/791-3957
Snail Mail	214 Elliot St., Suite 2, Brattleboro, VT 05301
Program Established	October 1998
Number of Affiliate Sites?	Confidential
Program Administration	In-house
Publically Traded?	No **Ticker:** N/A
Revenues 1998	Confidential
Competitors	"None online"
Commission Schedule	25% of sale
Return Days	N/A
Payment Schedule	Quarterly
Payment If Over	?
Type of Reporting	Online
Restrictions	Prefers like-minded websites (such as environmental issues/products, parenting/education, toys).
OK to Buy Through Link?	Yes
OK to Link to Competitors?	N/A
Highest Monthly Commission Paid to Date	Confidential
High Sales Incentives?	N/A
Additional Perks	N/A

Site Name	NetGrocer.com
URL	http://www.netgrocer.com
Type of Goods or Services	Groceries, health and beauty aids, general merchandise.
Email:	mallen@netgrocer.com
Phone	732/745-1000
Snail Mail	1112 Corporate Road, North Brunswick, NJ 08902
Program Established	November 1998
Number of Affiliate Sites?	1,100—June 1999
Program Administration	In-house
Publically Traded?	No **Ticker:** N/A
Revenues 1998	N/A
Competitors	
Commission Schedule	5% ($30 maximum per customer)
Return Days	No
Payment Schedule	Quarterly
Payment If Over	$100
Type of Reporting	Online
Restrictions	
OK to Buy Through Link?	Yes
OK to Link to Competitors?	No
Highest Monthly Commission Paid to Date	N/A
High Sales Incentives?	N/A
Additional Perks	N/A

Site Name	Network Solutions
URL	www.networksolutions.com
Type of Goods or Services	Web address (domain name) registration services, email, and one-page Web site.
Email:	affiliates@netsol.com
Phone	888/642-9675
Snail Mail	505 Huntmar Park Drive Herndon, VA 20170-5139
Program Established	October 1998
Number of Affiliate Sites?	16,000—June 1999
Program Administration	Be Free
Publically Traded?	Yes **Ticker:** NSOL
Revenues 1998	$93,652,000
Competitors	Register.com, America Online, Melbourne IT/Internet Names Australia, France Telecom/Oleone, Internet Council of Registrars (Core)
Commission Schedule	10% $0-$1,000 12% $1,001-$2,500 14% $2,501+
Return Days	N/A
Payment Schedule	Quarterly
Payment If Over	$100
Type of Reporting	Online via Be Free
Restrictions	
OK to Buy Through Link?	Yes
OK to Link to Competitors?	Yes
Highest Monthly Commission Paid to Date	$2,234.00/quarter
High Sales Incentives?	N/A
Additional Perks	Quarterly sales contests

Site Name	NextCard Internet Visa
URL	http://www.nextcard.com
Type of Goods or Services	Internet credit card
Email:	affiliates@nextcard.com
Phone	
Snail Mail	NextCard Affiliate Network 595 Market St., Suite 1800 San Francisco, CA 94105
Program Established	May 1999 (new program launched)
Number of Affiliate Sites?	14,000—May 1999
Program Administration	In-house
Publically Traded?	Yes **Ticker:** NXCD
Revenues 1998	$2 million
Competitors	MBNA, NetBank
Commission Schedule	At least $20 per sale
Return Days	N/A
Payment Schedule	Quarterly/Monthly (if over $50)
Payment If Over	$50
Type of Reporting	Weekly email
Restrictions	
OK to Buy Through Link?	Yes
OK to Link to Competitors?	Yes
Highest Monthly	
Commission Paid to Date	$17,760
High Sales Incentives?	Gold and Platinum Affiliate levels are $25 and $30 respectively.
Additional Perks	Customized banners and product offerings, Direct Deposit (coming soon).

Site Name	Omaha Steaks
URL	www.omahasteaks.com
Type of Goods or Services	Gourmet Foods
Email:	info@omahasteaks.com
Phone	800/960-8400
Snail Mail	10909 John Galt Boulevard, Omaha, NE 68137
Program Established	September 1997
Number of Affiliate Sites?	4,400+ —May 1999
Program Administration	LinkShare
Publically Traded?	No **Ticker:** N/A
Revenues 1998	N/A
Competitors	
Commission Schedule	7%
Return Days	0
Payment Schedule	Monthly
Payment If Over	$20
Type of Reporting	Online via LinkShare
Restrictions	
OK to Buy Through Link?	Yes
OK to Link to Competitors?	N/A
Highest Monthly	
Commission Paid to Date	N/A
High Sales Incentives?	N/A
Additional Perks	Free gift with purchase

Site Name	One & Only Network
URL	http://www.oneandonlynetwork.com/
Type of Goods or Services	Currently classifieds (including personal ads and auctions), moving towards a broad ecommerce network.
Email:	tech@oneandonly.com
Phone	214/827-2262
Snail Mail	5307 E. Mockingbird Lane, Ste. 102, Dallas, TX 75206
Program Established	May 1997
Number of Affiliate Sites?	over 105,000—June 1999
Program Administration	In-house
Publically Traded?	No **Ticker:** N/A
Revenues 1998	Grew 500% in 1998 over 1997. Q1 99 was1.8MM
Competitors	
Commission Schedule	15% + 33% of referral network associate's commissions. Opportunity plus (two-tier marketing network) associates receive an amount equal to 33% of the commissions earned by associates that they refer to the network.
Return Days	N/A
Payment Schedule	Monthly
Payment If Over	No minimum requirement
Type of Reporting	Real time online and weekly mail
Restrictions	
OK to Buy Through Link?	No
OK to Link to Competitors?	Yes
Highest Monthly Commission Paid to Date	$19,000
High Sales Incentives?	N/A
Additional Perks	Monthly promotions. Current examples include a $4 bounty for any new web masters recruited to the network, $1.50 for every Utrade (auction product) registered user that signs up via the affiliate site. Traffic contests with prize giveaways, such as trips, TVs, CD players, etc.

Site Name	OutdoorDecor.com
URL	http://www.outdoordecor.com
Type of Goods or Services	Outdoor home and garden products, including: sundials, weathervanes, address markers, and mailboxes.
Email:	sales@arthurwilbur.com
Phone	888/651-0113
Snail Mail	PO Box 3089, Tuscaloosa, AL 35403-3089
Program Established	August 1998
Number of Affiliate Sites?	475—May 1999
Program Administration	3rd party
Publically Traded?	No **Ticker:** N/A
Revenues 1998	$25,000
Competitors	Garden.com, LandscapeUSA.com
Commission Schedule	8%
Return Days	0
Payment Schedule	Monthly
Payment If Over	$10
Type of Reporting	Online
Restrictions	
OK to Buy Through Link?	Yes (for retail only)
OK to Link to Competitors?	Yes
Highest Monthly Commission Paid to Date	$63.51
High Sales Incentives?	N/A
Additional Perks	N/A

Site Name	Outpost.com (formerly Cyberian Outpost)
URL	http://www.outpost.com
Type of Goods or Services	Computer hardware, software, peripherals and accessories
Email:	affiliates@outpost.com
Phone	860/927-2050
Snail Mail	23 North Main St., Kent, CT 06757
Program Established	November 1997
Number of Affiliate Sites?	75,000—June 1999
Program Administration	LinkShare
Publically Traded?	Yes **Ticker:** COOL
Revenues 1998	N/A
Competitors	Egghead, Buy.com, Beyond.com, CDW
Commission Schedule	3% cash or 5% store credit
Return Days	4 hours
Payment Schedule	Monthly
Payment If Over	$100
Type of Reporting	Online via LinkShare
Restrictions	
OK to Buy Through Link?	Yes
OK to Link to Competitors?	Yes
Highest Monthly Commission Paid to Date	N/A
High Sales Incentives?	Tiered compensation plan and one-to-one account management
Additional Perks	N/A

Site Name	PC Flowers & Gifts
URL	http://www.pcflowers.com
Type of Goods or Services	Flowers and gifts
Email:	
Phone	203/977-8582
Snail Mail	2001 West Main St., Suite 175, Stamford, CT 06902
Program Established	October 1994
Number of Affiliate Sites?	1,800 co-branded sites/413 affiliate sites—April 1999
Program Administration	Cobranded—in-house/Affiliate—Commission Junction
Publically Traded?	No **Ticker:** N/A
Revenues 1998	N/A
Competitors	Proflowers.com, 1-800-FLOWERS.com, others
Commission Schedule	8%—Cobranding program 6%—Affiliate program
Return Days	N/A
Payment Schedule	Cobranded—Quarterly/Affiliate—Monthly
Payment If Over	Cobranded—$50/Affiliate—CJ (aggregate) check
Type of Reporting	Cobranded—hard copy-email/Affiliate—Online via CJ
Restrictions	
OK to Buy Through Link?	Yes
OK to Link to Competitors?	Yes
Highest Monthly	
Commission Paid to Date	N/A
High Sales Incentives?	High sales from affiliates can result in upgrade to our cobranding program.
Additional Perks	Cobrand program: unique URL for site; no affiliate codes to remember; account Executive assigned to guide partners.

Site Name	PetQuarters
URL	http://www.petquarters.com
Type of Goods or Services	Pet supply store
Email:	info@ecomworks.com
Phone	1-800-PET-Nett
Snail Mail	PO Box 410, Lonoke, AR 72086
Program Established	February 1999
Number of Affiliate Sites?	N/A
Program Administration	LinkShare/EcomWorks
Publically Traded?	Yes **Ticker:** PDEN
Revenues 1998	N/A
Competitors	Pets.com
Commission Schedule	7.5%
Return Days	45
Payment Schedule	Quarterly
Payment If Over	$100
Type of Reporting	Online via LinkShare
Restrictions	
OK to Buy Through Link?	Yes
OK to Link to Competitors?	No
Highest Monthly Commission Paid to Date	N/A
High Sales Incentives?	N/A
Additional Perks	N/A

Site Name	PlanetRx
URL	http://www.planetrx.com/
Type of Goods or Services	Pharmacy
Email:	affiliates@planetrx.com
Phone	650/616-1521
Snail Mail	349 Oyster Point Blvd., Suite 201 South San Francisco, CA 94080
Program Established	May 1999
Number of Affiliate Sites?	2,300—June 1999
Program Administration	Be Free/in-house outreach, and management
Publically Traded?	No **Ticker:** N/A
Revenues 1998	N/A
Competitors	Drugstore.com
Commission Schedule	25% special promotion, 15% base, $5 bounty for new customers
Return Days	N/A
Payment Schedule	Quarterly
Payment If Over	$50
Type of Reporting	Online via Be Free
Restrictions	
OK to Buy Through Link?	Yes
OK to Link to Competitors?	Yes
Highest Monthly Commission Paid to Date	N/A
High Sales Incentives?	N/A
Additional Perks	N/A

Site Name	Portico / myTalk
URL	www.genmagic.com/portico www.mytalk.com
Type of Goods or Services	Virtual Assistant (Portico) Free email reader (myTalk)
Email:	affiliate@genmagic.com
Phone	888/443-5604
Snail Mail	420 North Mary, 3/F, Sunnyvale, CA 94086
Program Established	June 1999
Number of Affiliate Sites?	N/A
Program Administration	LinkShare/In-house
Publically Traded?	Yes **Ticker:** GMGC
Revenues 1998	N/A
Competitors	N/A
Commission Schedule	$20—Portico $1—myTalk
Return Days	10
Payment Schedule	Quarterly
Payment If Over	0
Type of Reporting	Online via LinkShare
Restrictions	
OK to Buy Through Link?	Yes
OK to Link to Competitors?	No
Highest Monthly Commission Paid to Date	N/A
High Sales Incentives?	Yes
Additional Perks	N/A

Site Name	priceline.com
URL	http://www.priceline.com/
Type of Goods or Services	E-commerce system where consumers name their own price for leisure airline tickets, hotel rooms, home mortgages and new cars.
Email:	bfaffiliate@priceline.com
Phone	800/840-3485
Snail Mail	5 High Ridge Park, Stamford, CT 06905
Program Established	May 1999
Number of Affiliate Sites?	brand new!
Program Administration	Be Free/In-house
Publically Traded?	Yes **Ticker:** PCLN
Revenues 1998	$35 million
Competitors	
Commission Schedule	$10 for the first qualified offer submitted into the system. Thereafter, $1 per qualified offer. The program is available for both hotel rooms and airline tickets.
Return Days	N/A
Payment Schedule	Quarterly
Payment If Over	$50
Type of Reporting	Online via Be Free
Restrictions	
OK to Buy Through Link?	Yes
OK to Link to Competitors?	Yes
Highest Monthly	
Commission Paid to Date	N/A
High Sales Incentives?	No
Additional Perks	Plans to launch promotional programs to encourage affiliates to promote heavily.

Site Name	ProActive Electronics
URL	http://www.proactiveelectronics.com
Type of Goods or Services	Electronics (primary focus on home entertainment), computers, and appliances
Email:	sales@proactiveelectronics.com
Phone	888/439-4514
Snail Mail	473 Cane Ct., Mt. Pleasant, SC 29466
Program Established	September 1998
Number of Affiliate Sites?	1,200+ —July 1999
Program Administration	ClickTrade
Publically Traded?	No **Ticker:** N/A
Revenues 1998	Undisclosed
Competitors	electronics.net, Value America, others
Commission Schedule	5% on sales Up to 7.5% for high volume accounts
Return Days	N/A
Payment Schedule	Monthly
Payment If Over	$25
Type of Reporting	Online—with 20-minute delay
Restrictions	
OK to Buy Through Link?	Yes
OK to Link to Competitors?	Yes
Highest Monthly Commission Paid to Date	$3,500
High Sales Incentives?	Yes, increase percentages on future sales
Additional Perks	New program due to launch in Q1/2000 that will let affiliates set their own price. Affiliate will earn 5% on the normal sales price plus 95% of the additional markup. Affiliates will build their own stores and set their own prices while using LobsterNet's inventory and private label order processing system to ship to the customer.

Site Name	Proflowers.com
URL	http://www.proflowers.com
Type of Goods or Services	Fresh flowers and bouquets
Email:	info@proflowers.com
Phone	619/729-2800, 800/PROFLOWers (776-3569)
Snail Mail	7863 Girard Ave., Suite 302, La Jolla, CA 92037
Program Established	August 1998
Number of Affiliate Sites?	18,000—May 1999
Program Administration	Be Free
Publically Traded?	No Ticker: N/A
Revenues 1998	N/A
Competitors	1-800-FLOWERS, pcflowers.com
Commission Schedule	10%-12% At various times, the company has increased the commission rate (to as high as 20%).
Return Days	N/A
Payment Schedule	Quarterly
Payment If Over	$100
Type of Reporting	Online via Be Free
Restrictions	
OK to Buy Through Link?	Yes
OK to Link to Competitors?	Yes
Highest Monthly Commission Paid to Date	over $1,000
High Sales Incentives?	N/A
Additional Perks	N/A

Site Name	Publishers Clearing House
URL	www.pch.com
Type of Goods or Services	Magazine Sales, Sweepstakes
Email:	cashin@pch.com
Phone	516/944/4628
Snail Mail	101 Channel Drive, Port Washington, NY 11050
Program Established	November 15, 1998
Number of Affiliate Sites?	4,000—May 1999
Program Administration	LinkShare
Publically Traded?	No **Ticker:** N/A
Revenues 1998	N/A
Competitors	Enews.com, other subscription services
Commission Schedule	15-20% Sliding Scale 1st 2,020 affiliates locked in at 20%
Return Days	30
Payment Schedule	Quarterly
Payment If Over	$50
Type of Reporting	Online via LinkShare
Restrictions	Commission only on magazines
OK to Buy Through Link?	Yes
OK to Link to Competitors?	Yes
Highest Monthly Commission Paid to Date	N/A
High Sales Incentives?	Private higher commission offers for high sales sites.
Additional Perks	Free magazine w/ first $100 in sales Exclusive affiliate contests Separate web section dedicated to affiliates with archived newsletters, selling tips, and direct login to account

Site Name	QSPACE (formerly iCreditReport)
URL	http://www.qspace.com
Type of Goods or Services	Online real-time consumer credit reports products and personal financial services.
Email:	affiliate@icreditreport.com
Phone	415/882-9597
Snail Mail	425 Second St., Second Floor, San Francisco, CA 94107
Program Established	December 1998
Number of Affiliate Sites?	30,000—May 1999
Program Administration	Be Free
Publically Traded?	No **Ticker:** N/A
Revenues 1998	N/A
Competitors	
Commission Schedule	10% on sales
Return Days	N/A
Payment Schedule	Quarterly
Payment If Over	$50
Type of Reporting	Online via Be Free
Restrictions	
OK to Buy Through Link?	Yes
OK to Link to Competitors?	Yes
Highest Monthly Commission Paid to Date	"a few thousand dollars!"
High Sales Incentives?	N/A
Additional Perks	Giveaways and sales incentives: A Creative Blaster Webcam was given to random affiliates in February, 1999 and a Y2K Millenium Beanie Baby was given to a lucky affiliate in March. Awarded a pair of airline tickets to affiliates that sold over 10 reports (April-June '99)

Site Name	Reel.com
URL	http://www.reel.com
Type of Goods or Services	Videos, DVDs, laserdiscs, proprietary information and reviews
Email:	producers@reel.com
Phone	510/549-3333
Snail Mail	1250 45th St., Suite 200, Emeryville, CA 94608
Program Established	February 1998
Number of Affiliate Sites?	110,000—September 1999
Program Administration	Be Free
Publically Traded?	Yes (subsidiary of Hollywood Ent.) **Ticker:** HLYW
Revenues 1998	
Competitors	Amazon.com, DVD Express
Commission Schedule	8% revenue share
Return Days	0
Payment Schedule	Quarterly
Payment If Over	$3 (option of collecting commissions each quarter)
Type of Reporting	Online via Be Free
Restrictions	
OK to Buy Through Link?	Yes
OK to Link to Competitors?	In most cases, yes.
Highest Monthly Commission Paid to Date	"Enough to keep them swimming in new videos!"
High Sales Incentives?	Premium Producers receive special sale notices and a separate e-mail address and contact person.
Additional Perks	Monthly contests where affiliates can win everything from movies to merchandise to home theaters.

Site Name	Seattle's Finest Gourmet Coffee
URL	http://www.seattlesfinest.com
Type of Goods or Services	Gourmet Arabica coffees
Email:	info@seattlesfinest.com
Phone	425/343-6801
Snail Mail	13413 NE 132nd St., Kirkland, WA 98034
Program Established	September 1998
Number of Affiliate Sites?	1,000+ —May 1999
Program Administration	In-house
Publically Traded?	No **Ticker:** N/A
Revenues 1998	N/A
Competitors	Starbucks, Peet's Coffee
Commission Schedule	20%
Return Days	30 days
Payment Schedule	Monthly
Payment If Over	$20.00
Type of Reporting	Online
Restrictions	
OK to Buy Through Link?	Yes
OK to Link to Competitors?	Yes
Highest Monthly Commission Paid to Date	$950
High Sales Incentives?	"Not as of yet"
Additional Perks	N/A

Site Name	SelfCare
URL	http://www.selfcare.com
Type of Goods or Services	Unique products for health and wellness
Email:	Custserv@SelfCare.com
Phone	800/816-1673
Snail Mail	2000 Powell St., Suite 1350, Emeryville, CA 94608
Program Established	June 1999
Number of Affiliate Sites?	1,000+ —June 1999
Program Administration	LinkShare/i-traffic, in—program management
Publically Traded?	No **Ticker:** N/A
Revenues 1998	N/A
Competitors	Drugstore.com, PlanetRx.com, MotherNature.com
Commission Schedule	15%
Return Days	7
Payment Schedule	Quarterly
Payment If Over	$50
Type of Reporting	Online via LinkShare
Restrictions	
OK to Buy Through Link?	Yes
OK to Link to Competitors?	Yes
Highest Monthly	
Commission Paid to Date	N/A
High Sales Incentives?	20% of sales
Additional Perks	N/A

Site Name	SendWine.com
URL	http://www.sendwine.com
Type of Goods or Services	Premium gifts including wine, port, champagne, seafood, and others (to be introduced by 3rd quarter 1999).
Email:	affiliates@send.com
Phone	781/895-0000
Snail Mail	470 Totten Pond Road, Waltham, MA 02451
Program Established	November 1998
Number of Affiliate Sites?	5,000—June 1999
Program Administration	Be Free
Publically Traded?	No **Ticker:** N/A
Revenues 1998	N/A
Competitors	wine.com, Liquor By Wire
Commission Schedule	1-15 orders—$7 commission per sale 16-30 orders—$10 commission per sale Over 31 orders—$13 commission per sale (Cumulative)
Return Days	N/A
Payment Schedule	Monthly
Payment If Over	$1
Type of Reporting	Online via Be Free
Restrictions	
OK to Buy Through Link?	Yes
OK to Link to Competitors?	Yes
Highest Monthly Commission Paid to Date	N/A
High Sales Incentives?	Sliding commission scale. Other incentives in development.
Additional Perks	N/A

Site Name	shades.com
URL	http://www.shades.com
Type of Goods or Services	sunglasses
Email:	pwadler@shades.com
Phone	781/235-8830
Snail Mail	18 Dukes Road, Wellesley, MA 02481
Program Established	January 1998
Number of Affiliate Sites?	7,571—June 1999
Program Administration	LinkShare
Publically Traded?	Yes (Sunglass Hut International) **Ticker:** RAYS
Revenues 1998	$1.2 million (Internet only)
Competitors	peepsun.com, abeam.com, sunglass2000.com, sunglasses.com
Commission Schedule	10% for smaller affiliates 12% for major affiliates 15% highest (for site providing millions of impressions)
Return Days	90
Payment Schedule	Quarterly
Payment If Over	$10
Type of Reporting	Online via LinkShare
Restrictions	Reserve the right to terminate any partner.
OK to Buy Through Link?	Yes
OK to Link to Competitors?	No (for most affiliates). Negotiable with major partners.
Highest Monthly Commission Paid to Date	$350
High Sales Incentives?	"Not yet"
Additional Perks	Major partners receive a discount buying products.

Site Name	sharperimage.com
URL	http://www.sharperimage.com
Type of Goods or Services	Gifts/gadgets/travel accessories/personal care/electronics
Email:	kgrant@sharperimage.com/ mhorne@sharperimage.com
Phone	415/445-6000
Snail Mail	650 Davis St., San Francisco, CA 94111
Program Established	April 1999
Number of Affiliate Sites?	4,300—July 1999
Program Administration	LinkShare
Publically Traded?	Yes **Ticker:** SHRP
Revenues 1998	$243,114,000
Competitors	1-800-FLOWERS.com, 911gifts.com, Amazon.com, eToys, other giftsellers
Commission Schedule	10% on sales in cash or 20% on sales in merchandise certificates
Return Days	0
Payment Schedule	Monthly
Payment If Over	$100
Type of Reporting	Online via LinkShare
Restrictions	"Your website must work."
OK to Buy Through Link?	Yes
OK to Link to Competitors?	Yes, although they prefer you didn't.
Highest Monthly Commission Paid to Date	
High Sales Incentives?	Currently, there are no special high volume sales incentive programs, but for sites that demonstrate a large volume of sales, "anything could happen."
Additional Perks	"You can do all your holiday shopping at one place and receive cash back! Plus you get to be associated with the ever cool sharperimage.com"

Site Name	Simon's Stamps
URL	http://www.simonstamp.com
Type of Goods or Services	Rubber stamps
Email:	alciere@simonstamp.com
Phone	800/437-4666 413/253-5501
Snail Mail	13 Railroad St., Amherst, MA 01002
Program Established	1998
Number of Affiliate Sites?	205—May 1999
Program Administration	ClickTrade
Publically Traded?	No **Ticker:** N/A
Revenues 1998	$300,000
Competitors	iprint
Commission Schedule	30% of net sale amount
Return Days	90
Payment Schedule	Monthly
Payment If Over	$25
Type of Reporting	Through ClickTrade
Restrictions	Sites subject to prior review.
OK to Buy Through Link?	Yes
OK to Link to Competitors?	Yes
Highest Monthly Commission Paid to Date	$107
High Sales Incentives?	N/A
Additional Perks	Commissions allowed on personal sales.

Site Name	SmarterKids.com
URL	http://www.smarterkids.com
Type of Goods or Services	Educational toys, software, games, and books
Email:	assa@smarterkids.com
Phone	781/449-7567 ext. 222
Snail Mail	SmarterKids.com, 200 Highland Ave., Needham, MA 02494
Program Established	March 1999
Number of Affiliate Sites?	3,034—May 1999
Program Administration	LinkShare/in-house
Publically Traded?	No **Ticker:** N/A
Revenues 1998	$2.4 million
Competitors	eToys, KBKids.com, Amazon.com, barnesandnoble.com
Commission Schedule	10% up to $1,000 in sales 12.5% $1,001–$2,500 in sales 15% over $2,501 in sales
Return Days	N/A
Payment Schedule	Quarterly/semiannually
Payment If Over	$100 (quarterly)/Balance (semiannually)
Type of Reporting	Online via LinkShare
Restrictions	
OK to Buy Through Link?	Yes
OK to Link to Competitors?	Yes
Highest Monthly Commission Paid to Date	$252.44
High Sales Incentives?	N/A
Additional Perks	Monthly newsletter with special offers to affiliates, i.e., free educational software.

Site Name	Sparks.com
URL	http://www.sparks.com
Type of Goods or Services	Greeting cards
Email:	hiten@sparks.com
Phone	415/642-6799 x126
Snail Mail	595 Newhall St., San Francisco, CA 94123
Program Established	March 1999
Number of Affiliate Sites?	2,500—May 1999
Program Administration	LinkShare
Publically Traded?	No **Ticker:** N/A
Revenues 1998	N/A
Competitors	
Commission Schedule	20%
Return Days	N/A
Payment Schedule	Quarterly
Payment If Over	$10.00
Type of Reporting	Online via LinkShare
Restrictions	Gift Certificate sales not included
OK to Buy Through Link?	Yes
OK to Link to Competitors?	Yes
Highest Monthly Commission Paid to Date	N/A
High Sales Incentives?	Higher commission basis
Additional Perks	N/A

Site Name	Superbuild.com
URL	http://www.superbuild.com
Type of Goods or Services	Home improvement supplies, tools
Email:	biz@superbuild.com
Phone	206/652-9848
Snail Mail	76 S. Washington St., Suite m101 Seattle, WA 98014
Program Established	December 1998
Number of Affiliate Sites?	4,000—June 1999
Program Administration	LinkShare
Publically Traded?	No **Ticker:** N/A
Revenues 1998	N/A
Competitors	Home Depot, Lowe's
Commission Schedule	10% Standard Affiliates Program 5% Premium Affiliates Program (cobranded)
Return Days	N/A
Payment Schedule	Quarterly
Payment If Over	$50
Type of Reporting	Online via LinkShare
Restrictions	
OK to Buy Through Link?	Yes
OK to Link to Competitors?	Yes—Standard No—Premium
Highest Monthly	
Commission Paid to Date	N/A
High Sales Incentives?	N/A
Additional Perks	N/A

Site Name	Swiss Army Depot
URL	www.swissarmydepot.com
Type of Goods or Services	Swiss Army knives, watches, sunglasses, gifts, and pens.
Email:	pwadler@shades.com
Phone	781/235-8830
Snail Mail	18 Dukes Road, Wellesley, MA 02481
Program Established	January 1998
Number of Affiliate Sites?	7,117—June 1999
Program Administration	LinkShare
Publically Traded?	Yes (Sunglass Hut International) **Ticker:** RAYS
Revenues 1998	$1.2 million (Internet only)
Competitors	
Commission Schedule	10% for smaller affiliates 12% for major partners 15% highest (for site providing millions of impressions)
Return Days	90
Payment Schedule	Monthly
Payment If Over	$5
Type of Reporting	Online via LinkShare
Restrictions	Reserve the right to terminate any partner.
OK to Buy Through Link?	Yes
OK to Link to Competitors?	No (for most affiliates). Negotiable with major partners.
Highest Monthly Commission Paid to Date	$325
High Sales Incentives?	"Not yet"
Additional Perks	Major partners receive a discount buying products.

Site Name	Tavolo (formerly Digital Chef)
URL	http://www.digitalchef.com
Type of Goods or Services	Specialty foods, kitchenwares
Email:	service@tavolo.com
Phone	1-800/700-7336
Snail Mail	2505 Kerner Blvd, San Rafael, CA 94901
Program Established	August 1998
Number of Affiliate Sites?	3,198—August 1999
Program Administration	Be Free
Publically Traded?	No **Ticker:** N/A
Revenues 1998	N/A
Competitors	Cooking.com
Commission Schedule	25% through December 31, 1999
Return Days	N/A
Payment Schedule	Monthly
Payment If Over	$100
Type of Reporting	Online via Be Free
Restrictions	Site must be in the United States
OK to Buy Through Link?	Yes
OK to Link to Competitors?	Yes
Highest Monthly Commission Paid to Date	N/A
High Sales Incentives?	N/A
Additional Perks	N/A

Site Name	T-Shirt King
URL	http://www.teeshirtking.com
Type of Goods or Services	T-shirts
Email:	Roy@t-shirtking.com
Phone	800/493-7887
Snail Mail	PO Box 2187, Chandler, AZ 85244
Program Established	May 1999 (new launch)
Number of Affiliate Sites?	800—June 1999
Program Administration	In-house
Publically Traded?	No **Ticker:** N/A
Revenues 1998	N/A
Competitors	
Commission Schedule	5% to 10% of gross sales
Return Days	90 days
Payment Schedule	Monthly
Payment If Over	No minimum
Type of Reporting	Online
Restrictions	
OK to Buy Through Link?	Yes
OK to Link to Competitors?	Yes
Highest Monthly Commission Paid to Date	N/A
High Sales Incentives?	No
Additional Perks	Affiliate Mall

Site Name	The LobsterNet
URL	http://www.thelobsternet.com
Type of Goods or Services	Gourmet foods, primarily lobster gift packages
Email:	sales@thelobsternet.com
Phone	800/360-9520
Snail Mail	473 Cane Ct., Mt. Pleasant, SC 29466
Program Established	September 1996
Number of Affiliate Sites?	675—June 1999
Program Administration	ClickTrade
Publically Traded?	No **Ticker:** N/A
Revenues 1998	N/A
Competitors	Various gourmet food etailers
Commission Schedule	5% on sales plus $0.04/click-through Up to 7.5% plus $0.04/click-through for high volume accounts
Return Days	N/A
Payment Schedule	Monthly
Payment If Over	$25
Type of Reporting	Online—with 20-minute delay
Restrictions	
OK to Buy Through Link?	Yes
OK to Link to Competitors?	Yes
Highest Monthly Commission Paid to Date	$1,800
High Sales Incentives?	Increased percentages on future sales.
Additional Perks	New program due to launch in Q1/2000 that will let affiliates set their own price. Affiliate will earn 5% on the normal sales price plus 95% of the additional markup. Affiliates will build their own stores and set their own prices while using LobsterNet's inventory and private label order processing system to ship to the customer.

Site Name	TransAct! Offer Network
URL	http://www.smartbiz.com/transact
Type of Goods or Services	Revenue sharing offers which require no sale to be made: includes free magazine trials, club memberships, etc.
Email:	irv@smartbiz.com
Phone	732/321-1924
Snail Mail	ALC Interactive 88 Orchard Road, CN-5219 Princeton, NJ 08543
Program Established	1996
Number of Affiliate Sites?	10,000
Program Administration	In-house
Publically Traded?	No **Ticker:** N/A
Revenues 1998	N/A
Competitors	
Commission Schedule	Each offer has a different payout amount; varies from 50 cents to $50
Return Days	N/A
Payment Schedule	Monthly?
Payment If Over	$50
Type of Reporting	Online
Restrictions	Must be in U.S. or Canada 15,000 visitors per month minimum
OK to Buy Through Link?	N/A
OK to Link to Competitors?	N/A
Highest Monthly	
Commission Paid to Date	$20,000
High Sales Incentives?	N/A
Additional Perks	Monthly contests with cash prizes of $50 to $500 per offer (most months)

Site Name	Ultimate Bulletin Board
URL	http://www.ultimatebb.com
Type of Goods or Services	Internet bulletin board software
Email:	info@ultimatebb.com
Phone	206/374-2398
Snail Mail	Infopop Corporation, PO Box 1861, North Bend, WA 98045
Program Established	1999
Number of Affiliate Sites?	500+ —July 1999
Program Administration	Commission Junction
Publically Traded?	No **Ticker:** N/A
Revenues 1998	N/A
Competitors	
Commission Schedule	15% of license fees
Return Days	N/A
Payment Schedule	Monthly
Payment If Over	Aggregate check Commission Junction
Type of Reporting	Online via Commission Junction
Restrictions	
OK to Buy Through Link?	N/A
OK to Link to Competitors?	N/A
Highest Monthly	
Commission Paid to Date	N/A
High Sales Incentives?	N/A
Additional Perks	N/A

Site Name	underneath.com
URL	http://www.underneath.com
Type of Goods or Services	Brand name intimate apparel for men and women
Email:	contact@underneath.com
Phone	888/565-4295
Snail Mail	2844 Centerville Hwy, SW, Snellville, GA 30078
Program Established	February 1999
Number of Affiliate Sites?	100+—May 1999
Program Administration	LinkShare
Publically Traded?	No **Ticker:** N/A
Revenues 1998	< $1 million
Competitors	barenecessities.com, onehanesplace.com, metromanusa.com
Commission Schedule	10% of sale subtotal (before shipping charges are added)
Return Days	90
Payment Schedule	Quarterly
Payment If Over	$50
Type of Reporting	Online via LinkShare
Restrictions	
OK to Buy Through Link?	Yes
OK to Link to Competitors?	Yes
Highest Monthly	
Commission Paid to Date	$600
High Sales Incentives?	"Not at this time, possibly higher percentage down the road."
Additional Perks	Free merchandise

Site Name	Value America
URL	www.valueamerica.com
Type of Goods or Services	Over 20 departments of products, including computers, electronics, software, office products.
Email:	jjohnson@valueamerica.com
Phone	804/817-7688
Snail Mail	2300 Commonwealth Drive Charlottesville, VA 22901
Program Established	March 1999
Number of Affiliate Sites?	25,000+ —June 1999
Program Administration	Be Free
Publically Traded?	Yes **Ticker:** VUSA
Revenues 1998	N/A
Competitors	
Commission Schedule	3-5% on all products, $25.00 Affiliate Minimum, Membership incentive
Return Days	14 days
Payment Schedule	30 days
Payment If Over	$25
Type of Reporting	Online via Be Free
Restrictions	Affiliate site validation
OK to Buy Through Link?	Yes
OK to Link to Competitors?	Yes
Highest Monthly Commission Paid to Date	N/A
High Sales Incentives?	Monthly prizes include: Weber grill, Disney World trip, RCA 60" TV, Napa trip, home portable spa & treadmill. Grand prize: 12 days/11 nights in Hawaii & Tahiti
Additional Perks	Affiliates can have customers complete the order on the Internet, but provide credit card information via phone and still receive credit. Free Value America membership for affiliates and customers to join.

Site Name	ValueClick
URL	http://www.valueclick.com
Type of Goods or Services	Click-through network
Email:	help@valueclick.com
Phone	877/825-8323 or 805/684-6060
Snail Mail	6450 Via Real, PO Box 5008 Carpinteria, CA 93014-5008
Program Established	June 1997
Number of Affiliate Sites?	13,000—July 1999
Program Administration	In-house
Publically Traded?	No **Ticker:** N/A
Revenues 1998	N/A
Competitors	Double Click, 24/7 Media, Flycast
Commission Schedule	Per click-through
	$.12—Affiliate (15,000 imp.) $.15—Premium (100,000 imp.) $.17—Advantage (1,000,000 imp.) $.17-$.25—Advantage Plus (1,000,000+imp.) $.01 per click—affiliate referral program
Return Days	N/A
Payment Schedule	Monthly
Payment If Over	$30
Type of Reporting	Online real-time and email (monthly)
Restrictions	Must be a named domain. 15,000 impressions per month minimum. At least 50% of content in English.
OK to Buy Through Link?	Yes
OK to Link to Competitors?	Yes
Highest Monthly Commission Paid to Date	$30,547
High Sales Incentives?	Higher commission schedule.
Additional Perks	Lots of trinkets.

Site Name	Verio Affiliates Program
URL	http://www.tabnet.com/affiliates
Type of Goods or Services	Domain Name Registration and Web hosting
Email:	jmeltzer@verio.net
Phone	888/932-7722 x1193 707/251-5193
Snail Mail	5 Financial Plaza, Suite 201, Napa CA 94558
Program Established	Summer 1998
Number of Affiliate Sites?	4,000+—May 1999
Program Administration	LinkShare
Publically Traded?	Yes **Ticker:** VRIO
Revenues 1998	N/A
Competitors	Many
Commission Schedule	$25 for Domain Name Registration $30 for Web hosting Additional services available shortly.
Return Days	N/A
Payment Schedule	Monthly
Payment If Over	$100
Type of Reporting	Online via LinkShare
Restrictions	
OK to Buy Through Link?	Yes
OK to Link to Competitors?	No
Highest Monthly	
Commission Paid to Date	$1,025
High Sales Incentives?	None right now, under review.
Additional Perks	None right now, under review.

Site Name	Web Cards
URL	http://www.printing.com
Type of Goods or Services	color Web site postcards, business cards
Email:	webcards@printing.com
Phone	800/352-2333
Snail Mail	417 Cleveland Ave., Plainfield, NJ 07060
Program Established	July 1997
Number of Affiliate Sites?	3,000—May 1999
Program Administration	In-house
Publically Traded?	No **Ticker:** N/A
Revenues 1998	$1.8 million
Competitors	
Commission Schedule	$1 per lead, 10% of orders
Return Days	30
Payment Schedule	Monthly
Payment If Over	$10
Type of Reporting	Online
Restrictions	Must be business oriented site—U.S., Canada, and Western Europe only
OK to Buy Through Link?	Yes
OK to Link to Competitors?	Yes
Highest Monthly	
Commission Paid to Date	$1,500
High Sales Incentives?	N/A
Additional Perks	N/A

Site Name	WholeFoods.com
URL	http://www.wholefoods.com
Type of Goods or Services	All natural and organic grocery, nutrition and body care items; on-line community (chats, forums); Whole Living Magazine (recipes, articles, information).
Email:	suzy.shelor@wholefoods.com
Phone	512/472-5949 ext. 219
Snail Mail	1111 West 24th, Austin, TX 78705
Program Established	June 1999
Number of Affiliate Sites?	1,568—June 1999
Program Administration	LinkShare
Publically Traded?	Wholly-owned subsidiary of WFMI **Ticker:** WMFI
Revenues 1998	$1.38 billion
Competitors	Grocery: Wild Oats. Nutrition: VitaminShoppe.com
Commission Schedule	13% commission—Grocery, household, gifts, and gear items 20% commission—Vitamins & minerals, supplements, herbs, homeopathy & flower essences, body care, aromatherapy and baby care merchandise
Return Days	5
Payment Schedule	Quarterly
Payment If Over	$10
Type of Reporting	Online via LinkShare
Restrictions	
OK to Buy Through Link?	Yes
OK to Link to Competitors?	Yes
Highest Monthly Commission Paid to Date	N/A
High Sales Incentives?	Yes
Additional Perks	Rewards to top performing affiliate sites.

Site Name	wine.com (formerly Virtual Vineyards)
URL	www.wine.com
Type of Goods or Services	Wine and gourmet food
Email:	affiliates@wine.com
Phone	650/919-1975
Snail Mail	3903 E. Bayshore Road, Suite 175 Palo Alto, CA 94303
Program Established	1998
Number of Affiliate Sites?	N/A
Program Administration	LinkShare
Publically Traded?	No **Ticker:** N/A
Revenues 1998	N/A
Competitors	SendWine.com, Liquor by Wire
Commission Schedule	Up to 8%
Return Days	10
Payment Schedule	Monthly
Payment If Over	$50
Type of Reporting	Online via LinkShare
Restrictions	
OK to Buy Through Link?	Yes
OK to Link to Competitors?	N/A
Highest Monthly Commission Paid to Date	N/A
High Sales Incentives?	Yes
Additional Perks	Yes

Site Name	XOOM.com
URL	http://www.xoom.com
Type of Goods or Services	Software, hardware, electronics, gifts, housewares, video, DVD, health, business
Email:	affiliate@xoom.com
Phone	415/288-2561
Snail Mail	300 Montgomery St., 3rd Floor San Francisco, CA 94104
Program Established	November 1998
Number of Affiliate Sites?	16,000—June 1999
Program Administration	Be Free
Publically Traded?	Yes **Ticker:** XMCM
Revenues 1998	
Competitors	Geocities, ValueAmerica
Commission Schedule	15%
Return Days	N/A
Payment Schedule	Monthly
Payment If Over	$0
Type of Reporting	Online via Be Free
Restrictions	
OK to Buy Through Link?	Yes
OK to Link to Competitors?	Yes
Highest Monthly	
Commission Paid to Date	$75
High Sales Incentives?	Contests and special increased commission promotions.
Additional Perks	Additional discounts on selected products to affiliates.

Index

About the Author

Daniel Gray is a computer specialist and bestselling author or more than ten books, including *Inside CorelDRAW!* (New Riders Publishing). He is a principal of GrayAreas51, a media relations/publishing company that specializes in the Internet. He has been recognized by Amazon.com as an Associate of the Month and as an Affiliate of the Month by PlanetRx.